What People Are Saying About *The Pause Principle*

"To thrive and to innovate in today's complex, globally connected world, leaders need sophisticated ways to step back to understand what they are facing within and outside themselves. *The Pause Principle* provides pragmatic resources for making the critical move from management efficiency to leadership excellence."

—Daniel Vasella, MD, Chairman, Novartis

"Effective leaders would do well to pause and absorb the wisdom that Cashman imparts in this profound book. *The Pause Principle* demonstrates why creative pauses are an absolutely essential ingredient for clearer, more innovative leadership in today's increasingly dynamic, warp-speed world."

—Paul A. Laudicina, Chairman and Managing Partner, AT Kearney, and author of
Beating the Global Odds

"Kevin Cashman's latest must-read book focuses on the essence of leadership: being consciously reflective before we act. Incorporating Cashman's ideas into your daily practices will transform you as a leader."

—Bill George, author of *True North*; Professor, Harvard Business School; and
former Chairman and CEO, Medtronic

"Leaders, like so many others, are suffering from hurry sickness—always going somewhere, never being anywhere. *The Pause Principle* is just the right prescription for slowing down, listening, and getting the clarity needed to lead in deep connection with vision and purpose."

—Richard Leider, founder and Chairman, The Inventure Group, and bestselling
author of *Repacking Your Bags* and *The Power of Purpose*

"Here a veteran coach shares his long experience to help busy executives deal with the question, *In my rush for success, how do I help my soul to breathe and my mind to renew?* His answer echoes an ancient tradition: withdraw and return; reflect and act. I recommend this book wholeheartedly to everyone who is trying to lead a better life."

—Dick Bolles, author of the bestselling career management book of all time,
What Color Is Your Parachute?

"Of the thousands writing leadership books, Kevin Cashman hits the mark. In their quest for speed and efficiency, many leaders fail to pause and ponder, losing perspective, performance capability, and the ability to sustain operations as a consequence. Cashman coaches leaders from madness to sanity, then to wisdom, wealth, and self-worth—the new triple bottom line."

—Ken Shelton, CEO and Editor, *Leadership* E...

D0958908

"Leadership is a continual process of stepping back to get new perspectives in order to step forward with greater innovation and impact. Cashman captures the essence of leading in our dynamic, global marketplace."
— **Paul Walsh, CEO, Diageo plc, and former Chairman and CEO, The Pillsbury Company**

"Cashman has cut through the leadership clutter and found the essence of elevating leadership excellence: pause to perform, pause to be on purpose, pause to innovate. It has freed me to make better decisions, push boundaries further, and be more present to myself and with my team."
— **Dr. Deborah Dunsire, CEO, Millennium: The Takeda Oncology Company**

"Leave it to Kevin Cashman to challenge us to stop...to dig deeper for purpose and relational connection, to journey beyond the limits of the known to the unknown, to bring more of our leadership potential forward. If you think pause is for the fainthearted, think again. Pause is for the brave-hearted, fearless, most innovative leaders."
— **Karen Kimsey-House, cofounder and CEO, The Coaches Training Institute, and coauthor of *Co-Active Coaching***

"As we've come to expect, Kevin Cashman has once again given us a fresh new way of looking at leadership. In this particular case, he's produced a primer on the principle of 'pause.' And more than just telling us why it matters, Cashman clearly shows us how we can apply this powerful and effective tool to help move our organizations forward."
— **David Shadovitz, Editor and Publisher, *Human Resource Executive***

"Leadership is tough, but with Cashman's *The Pause Principle*, you can make it a lot easier and more impactful. Get this book to sort through the leadership smog with clarity, purpose, and innovation!"
— **Michael Paxton, Chairman, Transport America, and former CEO, Chamilia and Häagen Dazs**

"Grab this book, pull up a chair, and spend some quality time you deserve with one of the best executive coaches out there today. Kevin Cashman's *The Pause Principle* delivers the wisdom we all need in this crazy, fast-paced world. You'll find your time with Cashman reaffirming, energizing, and rewarding."
— **Kevin D. Wilde, Chief Learning Officer, General Mills, and author of *Dancing with the Talent Stars***

THE PAUSE PRINCIPLE

ALSO BY KEVIN CASHMAN
Leadership from the Inside Out: Becoming a Leader for Life
Awakening the Leader Within: A Story of Transformation

THE
PAUSE
PRINCIPLE

Step Back to Lead Forward

KEVIN CASHMAN

Berrett–Koehler Publishers, Inc.
San Francisco
a BK Business book

Berrett-Koehler Publishers, Inc.
235 Montgomery Street, Suite 650
San Francisco, CA 94104-2916
Tel: (415) 288-0260 Fax: (415) 362-2512 www.bkconnection.com

Ordering Information
Quantity sales. Special discounts are available on quantity purchases by corporations, associations, and others. For details, contact the "Special Sales Department" at the Berrett-Koehler address above.
Individual sales. Berrett-Koehler publications are available through most bookstores and online resources. They can also be ordered directly from Berrett-Koehler: Tel: (800) 929-2929; Fax: (802) 864-7626; www.bkconnection.com
Orders for college textbook/course adoption use. Please contact Berrett-Koehler: Tel: (800) 929-2929; Fax: (802) 864-7626.
Orders by U.S. trade bookstores and wholesalers. Please contact Ingram Publisher Services, Tel: (800) 509-4887; Fax: (800) 838-1149; E-mail: customer.service@ingrampublisher services.com; or visit www.ingrampublisherservices.com/Ordering for details about electronic ordering.

Berrett-Koehler and the BK logo are registered trademarks of Berrett-Koehler Publishers, Inc.

Printed in the United States of America
Berrett-Koehler books are printed on long-lasting acid-free paper. When it is available, we choose paper that has been manufactured by environmentally responsible processes. These may include using trees grown in sustainable forests, incorporating recycled paper, minimizing chlorine in bleaching, or recycling the energy produced at the paper mill.

Library of Congress Cataloging-in-Publication Data
Cashman, Kevin.
The pause principle : step back to lead forward / Kevin Cashman.
 p. cm.
Includes bibliographical references and index.
ISBN 978-1-60994-532-9 (pbk.)
1. Leadership. 2. Opportunity. I. Title.
HD57.7.C374 2012
658.4'092--dc23   2012018168

First Edition
17 16 15 14 13   10 9 8 7 6 5 4 3

Edit: Thalia Publishing Services   Interior design: Laura Lind Design
Proofread: Henrietta Bensussen   Cover/jacket design: Barbara Haines
Index: Linda Webster   Art: Richard Sheppard Illustration
Production service: Linda Jupiter Productions

Dedicated to leaders on the authentic, purposeful journey from management speed and transaction to leadership significance and transformation.

To act with economy of effort and obtain maximum value, such is the way of the wise leader.

—Chuang Tzu

CONTENTS

AUTHOR'S NOTE: The Pause Principle   ix

CHAPTER ONE: Introducing The Pause Principle   1

CHAPTER TWO: Pause to Grow Personal Leadership   37

CHAPTER THREE: Pause to Grow Others   77

CHAPTER FOUR: Pause to Grow Cultures of Innovation   107

THREE AFTER WORDS: Pause It Forward . . .   131

Notes   135

Bibliography   144

Acknowledgments   147

Index   150

About the Author   161

AUTHOR'S NOTE:
THE PAUSE PRINCIPLE

The Pause Principle can be a book or a life-changing leadership experience. It is up to you. To convert this book from a page-turning intellectual exercise to a life-changing, transformative experience requires profound pause . . . an intentional, conscious stepping back to go deeply into yourself, your leadership, and the world you touch in order to lead forward with deliberate purpose. Take your time to slowly digest this book by savoring the ideas, diving into the questions presented, and by pondering the meaningful implications. If you do, you will activate the latent power of pause and embody its enriching properties versus merely placing another interesting book into your library.

So . . . take a breath . . . slow down, and let's begin the powerful, purpose-filled journey that *The Pause Principle* charts for us.

Chapter One

INTRODUCING
THE PAUSE PRINCIPLE®

SEVERAL YEARS AGO, I SIGNED BOOKS at BookExpo America at McCormick Place in Chicago. It is a huge event with thousands of people and hundreds of authors. Every half-hour or so, thirty-two authors step out from behind a velvet curtain to sign books at an elevated podium. Attendees line up in long rows and patiently wait to receive their signed copies. While it had a bit too much formality for my taste, it was still a big deal for me.

Lining up behind the curtain with the other thirty-one authors, I noticed that to my right was George Stephanopoulos, chief political correspondent for ABC News, formerly White House communications director and senior advisor for policy and strategy during President Bill Clinton's administration. Although George looked like a teenager, he was unfazed by the event—cool, calm, and collected, which was in complete contrast to my visible enthusiasm. When we took our spots at our elevated podiums, George's line was long. It went on forever, wrapping around the corner beyond our sight. My line of people numbered a paltry seven. At first, I cycled through reactive embarrassment, insecurity, and disbelief. I thought, "Am I in the correct spot?" Then, I paused. Stepping back for a moment,

I caught myself and reflected, "How do I best deal with this situation?" This short moment of reflection gave me renewed clarity and purpose. "This isn't about me. It's about those seven people, and I will graciously, generously give them my full attention." Once I made that shift, I had a great time. By connecting deeply, I learned a little about each individual, then I signed each book. It became a wonderful experience.

After a little while, I looked up at my line. A small miracle had happened. I now had a long line of people awaiting my signature. I glanced over at George, and his line had emptied. Apparently his books had not arrived, and he had been dashing off his signature on photos of himself as substitutes without taking much time to talk with people. Evidently, word had gotten out: "You want a photo or a personally signed book from Cashman?" Even George noticed the shift and said, "You must have a great book." I responded, "Sure is. You want a copy?" Feigning importance, I signed one for him. The truth is I felt bad for him. I wouldn't have been very happy if my books hadn't shown up, and clearly his disappointing circumstances helped turn the tide for me and created my surprising book wave. Reflecting on this example and the thousands of other intentional pauses I have had the privilege to witness with clients over the years, it has become clear: *Pause powers performance.*

How often do we miss these small but significant moments? These key opportunities that can unlock our hearts and minds, open us up, and connect us more deeply with others so that we can create something new and different. All too often, we allow ourselves to be carried away by our busyness. We are too hyperactive, too reactive to even notice the hidden value-creating dynamics waiting just under the surface within us and around us. Tethered to our smartphones, we are too caught up and distracted to take the time necessary to sort through complexity or to locate submerged purpose. In our urgent rush to get "there," we are going everywhere but being nowhere. Far too busy managing with transactive speed, we rarely step back to lead with transformative significance.

PAUSE TO LEAD FORWARD:
THE PARADOXICAL LEADERSHIP
BREAKTHROUGH

Too often, we take for granted our simplest yet most profound and transformative human capabilities. Sleep, for instance, is on the surface very simple. We lie down, sleep, and when we wake up, we have renewed energy, vitality, and perspective. Our superficial analysis of sleep says, "Yeah, no big deal. We rest and wake up. So what?" But take a moment to consider how profound sleep really is. Every night we go to sleep fatigued and possibly stressed from the day. Maybe we even have a little tightness or muscle ache somewhere in our body. When we awaken we feel completely rejuvenated. The muscle ache has gone away and the mental stress along with it. We feel energized physically, mentally, and emotionally.

Sleep is an amazing, natural capability for transformation. However, we can abuse this inherent gift with overwork, increased stress, and too much stimulation. Imagine how challenging our lives would be if we lost this ability to rest, heal, and restore. In extreme cases of overtaxation and hyper-fatigue, individuals experience burnout, serious illness requiring hospitalization or even death because the restorative process has been compromised by neglect. The French call this *surmenage*. Sleep is a natural, transformative process that cannot be ignored if we hope to operate at peak levels of performance.

What sleep is to the mind and body, pause is to leadership and innovation. Pause transforms management into leadership and the status quo into new realities. Pause, the natural capability to step back in order to move forward with greater clarity, momentum, and impact, holds the creative power to reframe and refresh how we see ourselves and our relationships, our challenges, our capacities, our organizations and missions within a larger context. While losing touch with our ability to pause may be less obvious than losing our ability to rest, it can be just as devastating. Pause, like sleep, is a natural transformative process that cannot be ignored if we want to operate at peak levels of performance. In our fast-paced, achieve-more-now culture, the loss of pause potential is epidemic. For many it has been lost, ignored, or completely abandoned; for others it is unfamiliar, an unknown.

A prominent, hard-charging CEO came into my office one day, fell into a chair, released a deep sigh, and said, "I don't know how to put into words what I am feeling. People around me seem to think that I am doing well. My board is happy. But, I am feeling like I have lost my edge a bit. If I am totally transparent, I am not feeling quite as focused, passionate, energetic, and patient anymore. I even sometimes question why I am working so hard. What is the point?" As we spent time together, it became clear that he had slowly, over time, lost connection with his deeper sense of self, his relationships, and his purpose by overtaxing his drive and underinvesting in pause, reflection, and renewal. In the early stages of his career, he just pushed through situations with more and more force, drawing on his considerable will, intelligence, and experience to get through. Later, as he was rapidly expanding and elevating the scope of his responsibilities, he began to disconnect a bit from relationships, as well as from the generative pleasure of taking time to listen, support, and mentor others. Eventually, he got so caught up in doing and achieving that he rarely, if ever, stepped back to get a fresh perspective or consider a new alternative. He took less vacation, pulled back on his fitness regime, gained 20 pounds, was more short-tempered at home, and had this nagging, just-below-the-surface feeling: "Is this all there is?" Having lost touch with his natural pause potential, he coped by pushing harder with more will and control, unknowingly leaving behind his purpose-driven ability to inspire, restore, and innovate.

> *Managers assert drive and control to get things*
> *done; leaders pause to discover new ways of*
> *being and achieving.*

The demanding pace for global leaders has never been more challenging. Digitally connected every moment, we are increasingly tied to a 24-hour global clock. We are expected to perform continually in the face of global crises and multifaceted pressures, including downsizing and mergers, and the related stresses and expectations. The list of demands, personal and professional, never ends. This is the "new normal." Could it be that going faster and driving harder are not the answers? Could there be another way to creatively sustain high performance? Could it be that the source of our real value as leaders might come from different thinking and different choices rather than from perpetuation of the incessant pace we are straining to maintain?

Paying Attention to the Wisdom of Experience

I had the privilege of sharing some precious time with a colleague who was terminally ill. Aware of the compression of time, we dove into some authentic conversations about life. At one point, I got the courage to ask him, "Bob, what do you want leaders to never forget?" His wise response was, "Never forget to slow down, connect with people, and do something that is meaningful. Never go so fast that you forget that love and service make life worth living." Slow down? Meaning? Love? Service? As Bob faced his mortality, he had deeper clarity about what brings authentic vitality to living.

David, a seventy-four-year-old chairman of a public company, also shared his life-leadership wisdom: "Early in our careers we use our drive, energy, and ambition to propel us through the ranks. We make things happen. However, as we advance, and if we are self-aware, life begins to teach us new lessons—lessons of humility, reliance on others, and lessons that the whole . . . the bigger picture . . . is more important than we are. Why? The sheer scale and complexity of responsibilities, as well as the consequences to people are too challenging to go it alone. The earlier we learn to view life from this different perspective, the sooner we can line up with what's most important and figure out how to make our best contribution. If we don't learn these more people-centered, service-driven lessons until later, our path is much harsher. We spend our energies in battles for control, dominance, and the self-focused drive required to win rather than invested in meaningful service. Step back often. Reflect, and become more aware of yourself, your colleagues, and your mission. The earlier you do this in your career the more productive and fulfilling your leadership and your life will be."

FLIPPING THE
VUCA FORCES

For several years, I had the privilege of being a keynote speaker at one of the Army War College's leadership programs. I was humbled by how much I learned there, particularly about character-driven leadership and a potent perspective of our world called "VUCA." Borrowing this term from the Army War College, Bob Johansen, ten-year forecaster and author of *Get There Early* and *Leaders Make the Future*, has characterized the speed- and action-oriented, fast-changing, demanding world we lead in today as a "VUCA world: Volatile; Unpredictable; Complex; Ambiguous." Our addiction to action, our busy-ness, our preoccupation with incessant distractions and pursuit of the ubiquitous "more" in our 24/7, constantly connected, globally caffeinated culture conspire to diminish rather than strengthen our leadership capacities. We challenge ourselves to keep up, even hasten the grueling pace, and, frankly, we rationalize that it comes with the territory. Paradoxically, the job of leaders is to bring clarity to all this chaos. Warren Bennis mentors, "Leaders bring clarity and hope." No easy task in the vortex of VUCA.

Johansen contends that we have "to flip the VUCA forces to terms that create possibilities and redefine VUCA as: Vision; Understanding; Clarity; Agility." We agree. But, how do we bring about this transformation? Pause—a step back to lead forward—a transformative, pragmatic, albeit paradoxical principle for sorting through complexity and coming into conscious connection with what is important. Daniel Vasella, M.D., chairman of Novartis, who has been acknowledged as one of the most innovative leaders in the life sciences business in history and navigated the firm as CEO for more than fifteen years to its current status as a $58 billion life sciences powerhouse, shared with me, "Pause gives room to oneself and to others. It allows the digestion of things both conceptual, and emotional. Pause can be a way to sense-making by bringing together a more integrated, complete picture of what is happening in and around us."

For most leaders, at first glance, pausing to elevate performance is incongruous with their leadership DNA, especially for the most productive, highest achievers. Over the past thirty years of coaching CEOs, senior teams, and senior leaders around the globe, I have lost track of the number of times a high-achieving leader turned to me and asked, "Kevin, how can we step up to achieve more?" To their surprise and discomfort, I often recommend stepping back—pausing—but, because it is antithetical to what they have always done, they insist, "We don't need to *pause* more, we need to *do* more."

Why would pragmatic, hard-charging, achievement-driven leaders pause in order to accelerate performance and growth? Put simply, that is exactly what is needed to sort through complexity and then drive performance to the next level. If leaders today do not step back to gain fresh perspective and to transcend the immediacies of life, we will continue to crash economically, personally, and collectively. Our downside survival and upside innovation depend on transformative pause. Certainly, we need to do more to meet the demands of high-performance, complex problems, and innovation, but in today's world the *doing needs to be new and different.*

CREATING A
NEW NORMAL

Pause is a universal principle inherent in living, creative systems. It is part of the order, value, and growth that arises from slowing down and stepping back. In physics, it is the second Law of Thermodynamics: *As activity lessens, order increases.* The Pause Principle is present in economies, physiologies, ecologies, communities, organizations, and nations. We observe pause on the macro and the micro levels as a principle of life and leadership, a natural part of the continuum that catalyzes growth, innovation, and transformation. Like any valuable resource, yet unrecognized and therefore neglected, we have to explore and discover its pragmatic uses in order to experience its value-creating impact. Additionally, we need to learn to tap into pause, incorporating it in our lives and leadership, and leveraging it as a powerful resource, an innovation in and of itself.

The Pause Principle is the conscious, intentional process of stepping back, within ourselves and outside of ourselves, to lead forward with greater authen-

ticity, purpose, and contribution. This value-creating methodology allows more examination, higher-order logic, rational analysis, more profound questioning, deeper listening, higher-quality presence, broader perspective, greater openness to diverse thinking and input, and ultimately more impactful, influential, and innovative action.

> ### *Paradoxically, pause powers*
> ### *purposeful performance.*

Daniel Kahneman, psychologist, Nobel Prize winner in economic sciences, and author of *Thinking, Fast and Slow*, has discerned two critical systems that determine the way we think. He counsels us to be careful with our "fast thinking," the overconfident system that is absolutely sure of opinions, impressions, and judgment. This part of our mind generates ideas quickly without much consideration. When we think fast in complex or new situations, we unknowingly limit our options to what we know from the past or habituated patterns. This is dangerous in a VUCA world, which requires more forward-looking agility at every turn. As Kahneman says, "We are normally blind about our own blindness. We're generally overconfident in our opinions and our impressions and judgments. We exaggerate how knowable the world is. . . . What psychology and behavioral economics have shown is that people don't think very carefully."

Incorporating pause as a best practice can change that. Ron James, CEO, Center for Ethical Business Cultures, University of St. Thomas, explains:

> Our culture is based on speed and decisiveness, and it's tough to pause when you are always "on." Pausing for self-talk about what really matters and incorporating that in our decisions so we act with ethics and integrity is exactly what we need to do. We need to have a set of principles that guides our decisions and behavior. That begins with asking, "What do I stand for? What does the organization stand for?" Although it takes more time up front, pause allows for a richer decision, engages others, and creates a sense of power and early buy-in that impacts execution.

Leaders, especially, when faced with complexity and ambiguity, need to pause and "slow the picture down" to see multiple options, multiple futures more effectively.

Fast thinking is the domain of management transaction, whereas slow thinking is the leadership domain of strategic, innovative transformation.

Integrating Pause Points

If we are going to flip the VUCA forces to Vision, Understanding, Clarity, and Agility, pragmatic practices, or Pause Points, will help us focus our attention and our energy, to grow, to create, to solve problems, and to innovate. Pause Points will provide a way to instill a consistent, intentional manner for reflection by:

- Building self-awareness and clarity of purpose
- Exploring new ideas
- Risking experimentation
- Questioning, listening, and synthesizing
- Challenging the status quo, within and around us

Taking steps back during the process of reading the book to consider Pause Points will integrate foundational, reliable structures into our leadership development experience. These Pause Points will help to make pause an intentional practice—a new normal—as the transformative benefits activate, show up, and multiply.

Pause can take many forms as practices in our lives. Some help us focus attention and deeper understanding on self-awareness through intentional learning and growth on our own or with our teams; others help us defocus, rest, connect, or become more resilient and more creative. Still other pause practices help us discern what deserves our attention within and outside of ourselves.

Of the 100+ leaders we interviewed, nearly every one told us that there is so much coming at us at once, we need to pause to figure out what is important and what is not. Pause Points, whether structured or spontaneous, can help us do that. They are tools to help us regain our balance, feel grounded, and centered. They can help us be accountable to our commitments, our mission, and to people. Pause Points can help us intentionally imbue generativity, innovation, and a sense of meaningful service in our cultures. These are powerful opportunities for flipping the VUCA forces and for achieving not merely higher performance, but lasting, value-creating impact. In *The Pause Principle*, you will discover and experience many Pause Points to take pause from principle to practice. Let's do our first Pause Point together.

Pause Point: Pause to Perform

Take a moment to envision your life at its optimal state of performance. Expand this vision beyond your career to all domains of your life. Imagine your career at its most purposeful and value creating ... your key relationships and family in deep connection and love ... your self-awareness genuine and authentic ... your creativity and innovation at their peaks ... your mind, body and spirit energized and enlivened. Then, ask yourself:

o What shifts did I make in myself and my life to get here?

o What new choices did I make to create these possibilities?

o How did I step back to see myself, others, my vocation, and my health in new ways?

o How did I pause more deeply into myself to gain deeper insight and perspective?

o How did I more deeply listen, be present, and connect to others at a new level?

o How did I step back to collaborate more synergistically with others to create the new and the different?

○ How did these powerful pauses help me to step forward and perform in new ways?

Go deeply into the questions that have the most resonance for you. Take your time. Resist the hyperactive temptation to rush through this opportunity to slow things down. . . . Pause to sort through the complexity and the fog to get clarity and insight.

TURNING DOWN THE NOISE AND TUNING IN

Daily runs, an intensive coaching and development program, a meditation practice, reflecting and pacing in a laboratory, or an annual strategic planning retreat—all are forms of pausing for growth, heightening awareness, catalyzing cognition, and aligning what is important. Pause can even catalyze our creativity. Scientists know little about how creativity works in the brain. One thing that is clear: "taking a break by going for a walk, taking a shower, or going for a drive . . . letting things percolate . . . helps ideas surface." Pausing or slowing down catalyzes those *Aha!* moments, those flashes of insight that come to you when you are not focusing on a problem, but instead taking a swim, walking to the train, or merely relaxing by a stream. As Wolfgang Amadeus Mozart wrote, "When I am, as it were, completely myself, entirely alone, and of good cheer—say traveling in a carriage or walking after a good meal . . . it is on such occasions that ideas flow best and most abundantly."

Jonah Lehrer, author of *Imagine: How Creativity Works*, says science tells us that creativity and imagination require both disciplined, focused effort and a sense of freedom and abandonment. "There is no universal prescription for creative thinking." Instead, there are a variety of processes. "A big epiphany relies on a very different set of brain structures than the editing that comes afterward." When he's really stuck, Lehrer says, "I think about all that research on moments of insight which suggest that insights are far more likely to arrive when we're relaxed, and better able to eavesdrop on the murmurs of the unconscious. Instead of staying at my desk, I go for a long walk." He quotes Einstein as saying "Creativity is the residue of time wasted," and says, "I guess you could say I've gotten much better at wasting time."

Although some creative solutions require conscious effort, others emerge when we rest or step back . . . pause in some way. What may appear as a little "time wasted," may be the vital field from which our next innovative idea arises. Even sleep or power naps have a measured impact on cognitive connections that can impact problem solving. Pause is our inherent tendency and our intentional practice to grow, to let new ideas emerge, to move beyond what is to gather insight, energy, and purpose.

FIGHTING FIRES
WITH PAUSE

But pausing, stepping back, is not only about defocusing or relaxing. Our most pragmatic and powerful pause practices for dealing with complexity, crises, and for innovating may be a practice of stepping back for intense, focused inquiry—questioning, experimenting, observing, listening, evaluating—a continuous loop of reflection and action followed by more disciplined reflection and action.

Researchers Michelle Barton and Kathleen Sutcliffe make a hard case for what business leaders can learn from firefighters, who put their lives on the line every day to battle wild fires and save lives. Their research convincingly showed that more successful outcomes occurred when leaders paused, stopped momentum to encourage fire-fighting teams to challenge the current strategy, voice concerns, examine all the current information, and determine the best course of action rather than persist in blind dedication to the original plan. Through intentional interruptions, team members questioned, spoke up, and did not defer to someone else's perceived expertise.

In "Learning When to Stop Momentum," published in *MIT Sloan Management Review*, the researchers tell us, "When engrossed in an action, we tend not to notice small problems that may grow into large ones.

To overcome dysfunctional momentum, we have to be interrupted or create an interruption ourselves . . . points at which we can ask: What's the story now? Is it the same story as before? If not, how has it changed? And how, if at all, should we adjust our actions?" They explain further, "Once we're fully engaged in our plans and activities, we have a tendency to continue what we're doing—that is, to resist changing our course even when redirection might be for the best."

Barton and Sutcliffe recommend developing "an attitude of wisdom" characterized by a practice of "situated humility," pausing for different perspectives, and questioning: "How might the future differ from our expectations? How might changes or problems in one part of the business unexpectedly affect other parts? What parts of the situation can't we see? Try to create healthy skepticism about what you know and a greater awareness of what you don't know." By pausing or creating interruptions, we create opportunities to engage and encourage team members to challenge the status quo, to speak up and voice concerns, and to be skeptical of perceived experts. It is a proactive way for leaders to let team members know that they are actively seeking all news—bad or good—and that they are open to diverse perspectives. These are recurring themes in what distinguishes a manager from a leader. *Managers tend to consistently execute well-formulated, time-tested approaches, while leaders tend to find new ways to step into changing circumstances.*

Leaders who pause to develop the agility required to dance with VUCA forces open up possibilities.

An Inner Knowing

Leaders must intentionally pause . . . slow things down . . . to access and develop the capability for what W. Brian Arthur, founding head of the Economics Program at the Santa Fe Institute, describes as a deeper level of cognition . . . a "knowing" that comes from inside yourself. He says that when faced with a complicated situation, ideally he would "observe, observe, observe and then simply retreat. . . . You wait and wait and let your experience well up into something appropriate. In a sense, there is no decision-making. What to do becomes obvious." This inner knowing comes from a place within us so it requires a deeper awareness and understanding of who we are.

My good friend and colleague, Richard Leider, is author of *The Power of Purpose*; his life's work is about living and leading connected to your purpose, your authentic self, and to what is truly meaningful. In his work, he sometimes refers to a deep pause as a "purpose moment." Richard is a committed practitioner of pause, and he guides others in pauses small and big. His annual "Back to the Rhythm" expedition in Tanzania is a big pause—one month on a walking safari, "off the grid," without cell phones, Internet, or e-mail. This is an experience for reconnecting with nature, the Earth, quiet, solitude, and to another way of living, as part of a sharing community, in order to also reconnect with what makes us feel genuine happiness. Disconnected from the demands of the VUCA world, we pause to reconnect with ourselves, "to quiet our own chatter," to listen to others around us in a simpler place, in a different world where it is more conducive to stepping back. By doing so, we connect again with our own heart and mind and really listen to our own voice about what is most important and meaningful, so we can then listen more genuinely and contribute more generously to others.

From Management to Leadership

One of the most challenging developmental shifts for executives is the evolution from management effectiveness to leadership excellence. Research has demonstrated that if managers do not make the critical development move to increased interpersonal collaboration and high-order strategic agility, they will plateau in their careers. The transition is one from expertise and control to authenticity and shared purpose. This crucial evolution requires sufficient, intentional pause to build self-awareness, foster team collaboration, and increase strategic innovation. Pause is a catalytic process that has the potential, if practiced consciously, to bring forth transformative shifts to move from management to leadership. Seven key shifts from management effectiveness to leadership excellence that we address in this book are

1. Moving from self-centeredness to self-awareness and service
2. Moving from people dominance and control to people development and liberation
3. Moving from complexity and confusion to clarity and hope
4. Moving from a presumption of knowing and expertise to listening and learning
5. Moving from heroic, unchallenged ideas to collaborative, constructive engagement
6. Moving from the status quo to curiosity, exploration, synthesis, and innovation
7. Moving from accuracy and efficiency to purpose and transformation

One of the primary contributions of this book is to discern precisely how specific types of pause can be the prime movers in the transformation from management to leadership.

WHAT DOES PRAGMATIC PAUSE LOOK LIKE?

Mike Paxton, former CEO of Häagen-Dazs, former president of Pillsbury and CEO of Chamilia, reenergizes with regular runs and time with his family. He sketches out complex situations to get clarity by writing them down because that helps him prepare when stepping forward with new initiatives. Steve Piersanti, founder and president, Berrett-Koehler Publishers, practices pause in multiple ways. At the beginning of every staff meeting, he asks for a moment of silence. He intentionally schedules meetings and sets meeting agendas so that they offer recurring opportunities to pause and thoughtfully consider all aspects of Berrett-Koehler's business. He, too, writes to gather his thoughts, reflect, and garner new understanding to clarify decisions.

David Rothenberger, M.D., surgeon at University of Minnesota, has partnered with clinicians across the Fairview Health System to share a powerful pause practice recently established for all surgical procedures. "Brief" is a few moments taken before every surgical procedure to make sure that everyone on the surgical team, everyone in the room understands why they are there, what the procedure is, and what their shared goal is. "Brief" connects everyone to the value of their individual roles, as well as to their combined impact as a team. In addition to reconnecting everyone to a deeper sense of purpose and meaning in their healing mission, it shifts their mind-set from a hero mentality to a collaborative one and serves the vital objective of increasing the percentages of more positive outcomes.

Karen Kimsey-House, cofounder and CEO of Coaches Training Institute, likes to build in a structure to reflect, create, and connect with vision, purpose, and direction. She takes retreats, sometimes as long as eleven days, "to stop, to be, and to reflect," because she returns with expanded vision and new ideas for direction. Rohinish Hooda, vice president, U.S. sales and marketing, Ethicon Biosurgery, Johnson & Johnson, incorporates a continuous practice of pausing to question and think. He has initiated BIG—Biosurgery Idea Gurus—as a way to bring together many people working in different aspects of biosurgery to pause to share ideas and gain different perspectives in hopes that this collaboration will energize and accelerate innovation.

Pablo Gaito, vice president of human resources, Cargill, has integrated a powerful practice he calls "Five-Minute Synchronization" to help everyone, whether physically in the room or virtually in the room from places around the globe, to be present at meetings. It begins with a moment of silence and includes a few minutes of focused, inspired thought. Pablo spends time with his family, maintains a fitness regime, and paints on canvas to restore. Jeff George, global head of Sandoz, practices meditation daily to balance his drive with deeper connection.

These leaders are conscious, pragmatic practitioners of pause, and we think they are examples of what is to come. In an article on reshaping the workplace for the *New York Times*, David Allen contends that we need more space, figuratively and literally, to counter "the dizzying number of [technological] options" that overwhelm us. He says that paradoxically they don't necessarily make us more productive. In fact, they are paralyzing. There is an antidote, "but it's not going to come from the usual quarters. To be successful in the new world of work, we need to create a structure for capturing, clarifying, and organizing all the forces that assail us; and to ensure time and space for thinking, reflecting and decision making."

THE LONG PAUSE

The very act of writing this book was born out of pause. It was originally conceived more than ten years ago as a result of working with my colleagues to help senior executives step back to see new dimensions of themselves, their organizations, their strategies, and their approaches to innovation. Our Executive to Leader Institute® and Chief Executive Institute® have literally been laboratories of pause in which we have observed thousands of leaders who "step back to lead forward." We observe, and they do, too, the transformative impact of pausing for three days of personal and organizational leadership growth. We discovered that pause is not merely a coaching technique, but a deep inherent life principle supporting all authentic transformation. Pause is woven into the very fabric of life and leadership. It is a principle, a cause-and-effect relationship, that paradoxically impacts progress the more deeply we step back into it.

Fortunately, *The Pause Principle* had a long gestation period to give it a chance to mature and develop. For several years, we practiced it in various forms, observed its effects, interviewed people about it, helped others to practice it, and conducted initial research. This long "pause into pause" gave it substance and pragmatism. Eventually, after four years, I service marked the concept, The Pause Principle, knowing I would one day pursue the project of writing the book. After five more years of study and reflection, I was ready to write. Because the pause was so long and so deep, the writing happened at surprising speed. Pause had worked its magic. Twelve months after beginning the writing, fueled by this ten-year period of reflective pause, the book was published and released. The ten-year period of pausing for reflection gave me the space for that deeper knowing, the welling up of experience and connection deep inside myself that W. Brian Arthur described. From this place of pause, the writing flowed and the book was created.

In the final stages of the manuscript, my wife Soraya and I decided to take a journey to visit the Dalai Lama and to explore sacred sites in India. I was excited about the trip but conflicted about it too. While I was looking forward to the spiritual renewal, I had been traveling extensively internationally during recent months for work and felt that the physical wear and tear of another trip with jet lag and time zone adjustment might be too much. Plus, I had so much writing to accomplish, and although I knew the experience would be inspiring, I was concerned that it might also be a distraction. Once we got to Delhi, we were thrust into an unexpected pause. Illness hit both of us full force, culminating in a hospital stay with beds side by side. We had to forego our visit to see the Dalai Lama. Understandably, we were disappointed. "How could this happen after we came all this way? Why?" Life had other plans; life wanted us to slow down . . . to stop. Surprisingly, it became one of the most creative, productive weeks of writing in my entire life. My body was slowed down. There was nowhere to go, nothing to do, plenty of time to reflect and write. The ten years of incubation produced many of the most important insights, connections, and content of this book. Looking back, I realize that we traveled to India with too much fatigue, too little pause, and life forced us to take a step back to recover our balance. As a result, I fortunately had the opening, the time and space to write. It was a veritable practice field to step back and lead forward.

Pause is an inherent, generative principle that is always there, always available to us. Either we consciously go to it, integrating it in our lives, or it comes to rescue us. Think about the many times you've felt the tug of pause . . . your intuition telling you to take a break, or to take another approach . . . and how many times you've ignored it until finally you could ignore it no longer.

A BIG BOLD PAUSE

São Paulo is Brazil's largest city and the eighth largest metropolis by population in the world. With more than 21 million people, it has multiple challenges, including pollution and overcrowding. In an attempt to make a dent in visual pollution and give Paulistanos a sense of space, São Paulo's leadership stepped back to ask a question: What might happen if we removed the print advertising from our city? This question led to a bold pause that showed up as bold action.

In 2007, the city's mayor passed the Clean City Law, banning advertising on billboards, the outside of buildings, buses, and trains. The law, which is controversial to some and innovative to others, rids the city of the incessant visual advertising that dominated its outdoor space. It is an attempt to transform the urban landscape, reduce stress, turn down the high level of visual pollution, give its residents and visitors a pause from a barrage of visual stimuli that consumed their attention and distracted them from the natural character of the city and its landscape.

Although the ban is not meant to be forever, the mayor said that it has given São Paulo a chance to step back to think about what they want, how they want to reintroduce advertising in a more regulated way. This bold pause gives the citizens a spacious opening to choose intentionally what they want their city to be. This temporary, thoughtful solution began with a bold question that challenged the status quo and led to an even bolder solution.

We create the future and optimize leadership potential in the silence and potency of pause.

"To Pause or Not to Pause?" That Is the Question

Leaders foster and accelerate growth: growth of revenue, growth of market share, growth of profit, growth of purpose, growth of innovation, growth of contribution. But the key questions to consider are "Where does all this growth originate? What is the prime mover of growth? What fuels growth in the first place?" Too often, we view growth as merely an external process, rarely pausing deeply to consider its source within us, within others, and within our organizations. We excel at measuring growth, but do we slow down, step back, and precisely look at where it comes from?

From my experience advising CEOs and senior executives on talent development and reviewing research on leadership development, I have come to the conclusion that there are three critical factors to optimizing individual and organizational leadership: *growing oneself, growing others,* and *growing an innovative culture.* Imagine your talent with the awareness to self-monitor and self-correct through change. Envision your key talent passionate and equipped to meet the current and emerging strategic needs. What might be possible when you and your talent are able to create a culture that is innovative, learning agile, and resilient to our VUCA world? Would you be very close to what you need to compete in today's world? I think so. The Pause Principle is organized around three growth principles represented by concentric circles: Grow Self, Grow Others, and Grow Cultures of Innovation.

Three Domains of Growth

"To Grow or Not to Grow?"
That Is the Other Question!

Growth is an inside-out and outside-in process of transformation beginning with inner self-growth and moving to growing others and growing innovative cultures. Most change begins with self-change, and most growth begins with self-growth. "To grow or not to grow" *is* the other question. No amount of growing others and growing a culture of innovation will compensate for lack of self-growth. As enterprise leaders, our capacity for organizational growth is directly proportional to our own growth. Before we can grow others with authenticity and purpose, we need to consider our own growth with authenticity and purpose. If we do, our development of others will be powerful, and the credibility we have gained with others will be well earned. When we aspire to become the leader we wish to see in our organization, we have a chance to accelerate the development of others, and ultimately the entire culture.

THE POWER OF QUESTIONS: THE LANGUAGE OF PAUSE

Not only is it paradoxical for leaders to pause, to step back rather than take immediate action, it is often paradoxical for leaders to question and challenge themselves. Questioning our choices is perceived as second-guessing, and in the norms of some cultures, that can be construed as weak. Authors Eric Vogt, Juanita Brown, and David Isaacs wrote in *The Art of Powerful Questions*:

> The aversion in our culture to asking creative questions is linked to an emphasis on finding quick fixes and an attachment to black/white, either/or thinking. In addition, the rapid pace of our lives and work doesn't often provide us with the opportunities to participate in reflective conversations in which we can explore catalytic questions and innovative possibilities before reaching key decisions. These factors, coupled with a prevailing belief that "real work" consists of detailed analysis, immediate decisions, and decisive action, contradict the perspective that effective "knowledge work" consists of asking profound questions and hosting wide-ranging strategic conversations on issues of substance.

Why question when we have all the answers, right? What might happen if instead of having all the answers, we had all the best questions to engage others, ourselves, and our enterprises in optimal discovery? What might be possible if we built a bank of compelling questions and a practice of asking them, using them to probe and learn and to unleash brilliance?

Questioning is perhaps the most powerful pause of all. Questioning is "the art of seeking new possibilities," the language of coaching, the language of innovation, and the language of dealing with complexity and crises.

Questions force a pause and propel us to a new level of thinking and new possibilities. *Effective managers are trained to have the most accurate answers, while leaders foster the skill to pose the most profound questions.*

Therefore, pause is a pragmatic practice of deep, reflective inquiry leading to purposeful change. A questioning and reflecting practice focuses attention on ideas to challenge. It unearths information, expands awareness and clarity, shines more light, and opens up the mind, heart, and will. The process catalyzes fast thinking and slow thinking—the cognitive skill of associating and generating connections and the more reflective, discerning mental activity. Pausing for inquiry also connects us inside-out and outside-in to our inner self, our character, and our purpose, as well as to others and to what is going on around us. It fuels our leadership capacities, our learning agility, and enhances our value-creating impact. As a personal practice, this methodology can accelerate our own growth and contribution. As a practice that permeates the organization, it can throw open the doorways of authentic innovation in the culture of our organization and accelerate the sustained growth of the enterprise. Pause is a pragmatic, transformational methodology that can be learned; yet this process of questioning, reflecting, and synthesizing is rarely taught.

In *The Innovator's DNA: Mastering the Five Skills of Disruptive Momentum*, Clayton Christensen and co-authors Jeff Dyer and Hal Gregersen lay out the five skills they have determined that innovators, including the late Steve Jobs, all have in common. Among these skills is an embodied practice of questioning. "Innovators are consummate questioners," they exclaim. They are also keen observers, experimenters, and networkers of ideas who make many associations. The "discovery skills," which are pausing skills at their core, are not beyond the ability or reach of CEOs and senior leaders; many just haven't had the practice developing the skill set. To develop our skills as innovators, we need to improve our discovery skills, beginning with our practice of pausing to probe and question. Then we can use this combination with our delivery or execution skills. Through pause, our execution skill will be more powerful because our discoveries are more profound. Through pause we get clear on what is important and why, then we drive to that outcome.

Innovation:
The New Leadership

Even before Steve Jobs passed away in October 2011, innovation was the hot topic. Jobs and Apple, the iPad, the iPhone, iTunes, Apple retail stores, and the new entrepreneurial industry of apps, as well as Pixar and Disney . . . almost anything he touched had become the iconic embodiment of creativity and innovation that transformed our lives. In fact, we could say that innovation has become the new leadership. Jobs's resignation as CEO of Apple and his death soon afterward provoked a global mournfulness for his loss, as well as a global curiosity and conversation about how to be innovative . . . how to "think like Steve." More important, leaders yearn to know how to imbue their organizational cultures with the spirit of innovation evident at Apple, Google, and other continuously innovating entities. Leaders aspire to join Jobs in "making a dent in the universe" in their own unique ways. They want to know not only how to cultivate new ideas but how to foster a culture that takes new ideas and turns them into innovations that transform people's lives.

Pausing for deep inquiry and questioning gives us the capacity to capitalize on disruptions and challenges to the status quo. Rather than viewing disruptions as threats, we can pause and proactively explore their possibilities. Pausing for questioning generates learning and innovation. Extending the questioning challenges accepted thinking and moves us from "what is" to "what might be." Persistent inquiry catalyzes synthesis and the emergence of something new from the intersections of opposing forces and glaring differences. Pausing is a methodology for proactively navigating toward openings, and a capacity for turning uncertainty and volatility to an advantage . . . an opening for something new to emerge.

If innovation is the new leadership, then pause is the new, transformative core competency for innovative breakthrough.

BRINGING CLARITY TO
COMPLEXITY

In his new book, *Beating the Global Odds: High Stakes Decision Making for Success*, Paul Laudicina, managing partner and chairman of the board of A. T. Kearney, writes:

> Not surprisingly, people (and organizations) everywhere are feeling disoriented, bewildered, and even paralyzed. From crisis and scandal to the proliferation of product choice and the relentless 24/7 "information smog" of always-on news, email, and social media, we are not feeling smarter and wiser. On the contrary, our ability to think and act decisively with the future in mind has diminished. Imagine having—at last—the entire knowledge of human civilization at your fingertips, and finding it basically gives you a migraine.

Reminding us of Gutenberg's press, the Dewey Decimal System, computers, and now Google, he explains that throughout our history we have developed ways to make the world's body of knowledge accessible to us. "All these things have helped to make possible that the immense and ongoing expansion of the world's body of knowledge is an asset to leverage, rather than an albatross around the neck."

But, what happens when that is no longer the case? Laudicina posits that we have arrived at a point where we cannot keep up for two reasons:

> First, with the geometric expansion of available knowledge and the increasing diversity of ways to deliver and access it, we are past the point where new tools can be developed in enough time to keep pace. The second is that, regardless of the capacity or technological sophistication of our tools, the volume and velocity of information increases geometrically, but our ability to understand and act upon that information explosion chugs behind linearly. No longer can the information surge be managed solely through superior organization. Rather, a wholesale new way of thinking, behaving, and discerning is necessary to manage and cope with the pace of change and disruption. In a sense, this

represents a new limit to the utility of technology—even the best systems will be limited by the capacity of individuals and society to usefully absorb the data surge and then, with wisdom, know what to do with it.

Laudicina says that he is not "advocating that you cut your cables and smash your smartphones." But he references Dr. Thomas Cooper, author and media analyst, who says that "the only healthy response to 'fast media' is a regular 'media fast'—a kind of detox for the mind." He reminds us that Steve Jobs "took the time out to get in touch with his inner self before going on to set the world on fire." In other words, perhaps the most valuable innovation we can make is the one that is most accessible to us. We can pause . . . step back . . . to see through the "information smog," to discern what is important and to gain deeper awareness and synthesis of information.

As leaders, too often we step forward with action to deal with complexity without first stepping back for the clarity we need. Our impulse to speed up and take action is driven by our intention to achieve, but our go-to approach—action and transaction—is often futile when dealing with increasing chaos and complexity. Unknowingly, our dedication to speed and action can be counterproductive. As the VUCA forces intensify, we have to consider learning how to step back to get clear so we can step forward with optimal contribution. Learning to bring clarity to complexity is an essential value-creating competency for leaders today. The research is loud and clear. Bob Eichinger and Michael Lombardo of Lominger International identified "dealing with ambiguity" as the most important leadership competency in shortest supply, and the Center for Creative Leadership backs this up with research showing that the number one issue facing senior leadership today is "dealing with complex challenges." I recently shared this research with a global CEO. His immediate response was insightful: "Actually, we do not need to 'manage complexity' or 'deal with ambiguity.'" Our job as leaders is to transform complexity and ambiguity into something that creates enduring value.

Slowing down amid the chaos is no easy task when we are accustomed to being rewarded for speed and action. Several years ago, I took a group of senior sales leaders of a global telecommunications company on an off-site retreat with the intention of dealing with complex issues. Based on our assessment of the group and their interests, we designed an array of experiences to accomplish this learning, including a very complex, challenging, multisport, problem-solving experience. When we were geared up and assembled for this outdoor activity, we began briefing everyone on the challenge. Suddenly, some of them jumped on their bikes, while others took off and started running in all directions. I shouted to them, "Where are you going?" Someone responded, "We don't know, but we're going now!" So eager to solve the problem and get to the goal, we too often head off with great intentions and drive but without a clear direction and an understanding of why. Tempering our drive to achieve with a commensurate *drive to pause* is crucial when facing our toughest, most complex leadership challenges.

The greater the complexity, the deeper the reflective pause required to convert the complex and ambiguous to the clear and meaningful. Pause helps us to move from the transactive or the hyperactive to the transformative.

Without sufficient, high-quality pause, the complexity of the VUCA forces becomes overwhelming as we try to cope by accelerating action or transaction. This attempt to manage versus lead our way out of the VUCA vortex seldom is successful. Ludwig Hantson, president, Baxter Bioscience, commenting on this crucial leadership dynamic shared with me, "Moving from management transaction which deals with noncomplex, unidimensional perspectives to leadership transformation which steps back to embrace complex, multidimensional realities is the key to innovation and value-added differentiation today." The following model illustrates this essential Pause Principle dynamic:

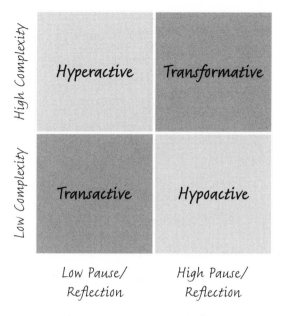

The Pause Principle Model

One of the key developmental shifts for moving from management effectiveness to leadership excellence is moving from the transactive and the hyperactive to the transformative by increasing the amount of high-quality pause and reflection, inside and out. If a situation is straightforward and requires action, not reflection, prolonged pause is not appropriate. If we find ourselves in this hypoactive state—dallying a little too long in pause—we need to push ourselves out of pause, or what may be hesitation, by telling ourselves, "Just make the best decision you can, and move on!"

The sweet spot of management effectiveness and leadership excellence is agilely flexing between the transactive and transformative depending on the degree of complexity. The developmental challenges are often in our hyperactive or hypoactive states when we are either pausing too little or too much. As one CEO shared with me, "The key to leadership is knowing precisely when to step forward and when to step back. Reflection is not an end in itself, but rather our unique human capability to process the difficult, the challenging, and the complex."

*Management effectiveness involves doing
more with greater efficiency and speed, while
leadership excellence involves doing differently
by slowing down to transform complexity
to clarity. Manage in low-complexity
situations; lead when facing high-complexity
environments.*

HESITATION:
A SIGNAL TO PAUSE

Too often we perceive hesitation and pause as the same. However, these two have subtle and distinct differences, and it is important to discern these differences. Hesitation, if recognized properly, can signal to us that a pause is in order . . . that we need to pay attention to a crucial sense-making response within us that has been provoked by the inner and outer complexity of a situation. At times, we may hesitate due to opposing forces we are facing. Other times, we may hesitate because we are confronting an inner or external fear. Occasionally, we hesitate because we do not have the information, knowledge, or experience required. We may feel insecure and need to sort out why we feel that way. We may hesitate because an impulsive emotional response needs to be examined. Once in a while, we hesitate because we simply do not know what to do or what to think in that moment. In each case, hesitation is a signal, a sign that stepping back to examine our internal and external situation is called for in order to avoid getting stuck or making a less than optimal, reactive response.

Conscious pause activates the deeper regions of our potential to meet immediate and future challenges. As Rollo May wrote, "Human freedom involves our capacity to pause, to choose the one response toward which we wish to throw our weight." Pause gives weight, *gravitas*, to leaders. Daniel Vasella, M.D., chairman of Novartis suggests, "A key question to ask ourselves about pause is, 'Where is it coming from?' Are we pausing due to anger, insecurity, passive aggression, or empathy, compassion, reflection, and insight to get a clearer perspective on things?"

Pause can power clarity and performance; it brings us closer to the self-actualizing zone where the potential for discernment, intelligence, and power can be optimized. The practice of pausing can give us the tools to be proactive, to take deliberate reflection and thoughtful action.

PAUSE POINT:
MOVING FROM HESITATION TO PAUSE,
THEN DELIBERATE ACTION

Think of a situation or a person that is causing you hesitation and anxiety in your career or personal life right now. What is the situation? Who is the person? What is the anxiety?

Close your eyes and deeply face this hesitant concern without judgment. Let the fears, feelings, disastrous scenarios come and go. Face it deeply and do not push it away. Observe your thoughts. Face the anxiety as it comes and goes. Feel the pressures in your body. Do not judge. Let the drama play out. Face the disaster scenario. Notice your beliefs, fears, biases, and memories. The more you observe, the deeper you will go. Be patient; watch and observe. Over time, as you move from anxiety to calmness, which might take a while, or even a couple of sessions, ask yourself:

o What was rational and irrational about my responses to this situation?

o What is the learning that could emerge from this?

o How could I approach this situation in a different manner? What is an alternative future?

o What is a new way of looking at myself and at this situation?

o What would be an elegant solution?

o What could I do differently today?

Stay with this process for a while. Sleep on it. Dream about it. Take a walk with it. Dwell on it while you drive the car or ride the train. A clearer perspective will emerge the more you step back and examine it.

Moving from reactive to proactive pause is a practice. Use your hesitation to signal that it is time to pause deeply. The art of leadership is recognizing hesitation as a calling to pause to ask the challenging questions and have the uncomfortable conversations within us and with others. As leaders, we pause to face ourselves, pause to face challenges, and pause to bring forth creative potential.

> *Managers speed up to increase efficiency;*
> *leaders slow down to connect to the*
> *meaningful, the important, and the*
> *innovative.*

As Margaret Wheatley says, "Thinking is the place where intelligent actions begin. We pause long enough to look more carefully at a situation, to see more of its character, to think about why it's happening, to notice how it's affecting us and others." All too often, we are so busy chasing down every leaf that is falling, we lose sight of the path that will bring us to a greater destination. Take the time to pause powerfully to lead powerfully.

HARNESSING DRIVE THROUGH PAUSE

Terry Bacon, founder of Lore International, a Korn/Ferry Company, and author of two groundbreaking books, *The Elements of Power* and *The Elements of Influence*, shared compelling research on the influencing dynamics of leaders. Bacon has found that leaders with high drive have ten times the influencing power of leaders with average drive. He also discovered that leaders with high credibility have four times the influence of leaders with average credibility. The implications of this research are huge. The greatest risks organizations and societies face today are leaders with high drive and low credibility. These self-focused leaders have huge influence *and* enormous destructive potential. The key to developing leaders today is finding ways to complement and balance high drive with humility, authenticity, credibility, collaboration, and service. Pause is the methodology to help move, via self-awareness and authenticity, from self-driven management to character-driven leadership. Stepping back to lead forward is a critical process of learning to lead as a whole person, harnessing our drive and talents to something much bigger and more important than our individual achievement.

HITTING THE VUCA WALL

I know from personal experience that letting go of my pause practices, especially when the pressure heats up, results in extremely painful consequences. A few years ago, I transitioned my long-held consulting firm, LeaderSource, into the Leadership and Talent Consulting arm of Korn/Ferry International, the largest executive search firm in the world. It was a great strategic move. Joining other outstanding firms, including Lominger International and Lore International, we formed a talent management powerhouse to complement Korn/Ferry's core practice in executive search. The growth was rapid as we hit $120 million in relatively short order. Sounds great, right? So what's the problem?

A wave of VUCA, what felt like a tsunami, flooded all aspects of my life. The business moved from one office in downtown Minneapolis to eighty offices across the globe, and suddenly I went from having twenty-five colleagues to several hundred. A big change, but also an exciting opportunity, and I welcomed it. In the midst of this major shift on the work and career front, I was dramatically deepening my relationship with Soraya. No problem. Right? Love is good. My energy was high with all this happiness. We became engaged. Soraya and Tahiel, now my son, moved to Minneapolis from thousands of miles away. We formed a new family, bought a house and remodeled it. Tahiel entered a new school, and to top things off, we incorporated a Golden Retriever puppy into the mix. By typical stress meters, that's quite a lot of change all at once, but still it felt relatively manageable, until the next wave came that made us feel like VUCA was filling up every corner of our lives.

A serious illness struck our family. Keeping up with the increased demands of a new worldwide company by day, worrying and being a caregiver at night, took me to an edge I hadn't felt in a long while. I was barely treading water. This major health crisis called upon all our resources, including our pause practices . . . reflection, meditation, exercise . . . and instead of maintaining them, we pulled back from them as we went into full-fledged crisis mode. Already drawn down because of multiplied new demands including more global travel, my resilience equity was depleting daily because I wasn't pausing for recovery and perspective. At one point during this overwhelming period, I remember being on a turbulent flight and feeling, "Okay. Take me now. I'm ready."

Realizing that I was at that edge stunned me and brought me to my senses. I reawakened to the significant value of incorporating my powerful pause practices into my life, especially at this challenging time, so that I could show up with more to invest and contribute for myself and everyone else on all fronts.

Losing or giving up the practice of pause is giving up our ability to restore and refresh, focus and connect, clarify and innovate—all of which are essential in our demanding lives. Fortunately, the VUCA forces subsided before I was totally spent. Even more fortunately, our family regained our strength, health, and resilience. We learned much from the experience, and as a tribute to all we learned, Soraya designed and supervised the building of a Pause Sanctuary in our home. This retreat space is a beautiful, peaceful place for respite—a haven—for writing, reflecting, meditating . . . pausing in all forms. It represents the sweet restoration of pause in our lives. Now married, Soraya and I no longer take the value of pause for granted; it saved our lives.

Step Back to Lead Forward: Seven Pause Practices

In the course of writing this book, we have conducted interviews and analyzed a multitude of research and case studies. From this work, we have isolated Seven Pause Practices that support the meta-pause principle: Step back to lead forward. Woven through the book, these Seven Pause Practices are the pragmatic ways to breathe life into each growth area: grow self, grow others, grow cultures of innovation. The applications are unique to each domain. The *Seven Pause Practices* culled from our research are

Pause Practice 1: Be On-Purpose

As Warren Bennis counsels, "Leaders remind people what is important." Meaning inspires us to "go beyond what is," to contribute something extraordinary. Purpose is the intersection of competency and contribution that aspires to achieve something bigger, something beyond us. Purpose gives context, drive, and meaning to personal growth, talent growth, and growth of innovation. It may be the most important, most far-reaching, transformative pause of all.

Pause Practice 2: Question and Listen

Questions are the probing language of pause, forcing us to step back, reframe, re-vision, and reconsider. Questions are the learning links that, over time, connect knowing to wisdom. Questions are the spades of curiosity that allow us to dig deeper foundations for personal, relational, and creative growth.

Listening is the receptive language of pause. Listening with authenticity opens up doorways to self-knowledge, understanding others and innovative possibilities; it introduces us to new ways of thinking, behaving, and seeing the world. Listening is the incubator for growing clarity out of complexity; it is the silent, pause-ful soul of transformative learning.

Pause Practice 3: Risk Experimentation

Managers minimize risk and experimentation to increase predictability; leaders monitor risk and accelerate experimentation to foster breakthrough. Stepping back to attempt the new and the different establishes the pathway to learning and discovery. If we hold onto the status quo and the tried-and-true, we are left with efficiency as our main source of value creation. However, when we experiment, we have a chance to foster entirely new ways to create value. Experimentation requires boldness and the courage to face failure and to leverage its potent learning. It challenges how we see ourselves and our world; it is the very essence of discovery. Risking experimentation is pausing at the edgy, uncomfortable intersection of current reality and future reality; leaders create the future through intelligent experimentation.

Pause Practice 4: Reflect and Synthesize

> *Managers analyze, judge, and decide to*
> *manage current realities; leaders reflect and*
> *synthesize to create new realities.*

As leaders, we tend to overanalyze, underreflect, and undersynthesize. Addicted to speed and action, we become transactive *deciders* versus transformative *synthesizers*. Great leaders take the time to incubate analysis to discover higher-order, more strategic, forward-thinking solutions. Reflective synthesis is equally important for leaders to develop self-awareness, talent awareness, and innovation breakthroughs. Reflection and synthesis hold the keys to unlock the doors of authenticity, transformation, and innovation.

Pause Practice 5: Consider Inside-Out and Outside-In Dynamics

Good leaders look outside themselves for strategic solutions; great leaders look inside themselves and outside themselves for enduring transformation.

Pause is a holistic, integrated process of considering dynamic forces within us and outside of us. The more we pause to consider both endogenic and exogenic forces, the more potential personal insight, talent insight, and strategic insight available. Pausing to more deeply consider internal and external information creates a greater likelihood for profound personal, strategic, interpersonal, and organization growth. Balancing our pause practices "to look inside" and "to look outside" is the pause-through needed for authentic, enduring breakthrough.

Pause Practice 6: Foster Generativity

A generative leader pauses to prepare the next generation more than he or she pauses for personal success. Generativity is the energy and enthusiasm we get by helping people to surpass us. It is the joy of giving, coaching, mentoring, and stretching people to go beyond us. Generativity is the joy of parents seeing their children elevating themselves; it is the joy of leaders multiplying their impact for future generations. Generative pause fosters a rich atmosphere for human potential to flourish.

Pause Practice 7: Be Authentic

There is no greater influential act than a leader authentically being the change he or she wishes to see in their organization. Once a leader becomes what she wants others to aspire to, the attractive force is irresistible and people rush in to engage and to contribute. Pausing to be more authentic with ourselves, with our people, and with what we aspire to create is critical to enduring value creation. Authenticity gives substance, realness, and value to everything it touches.

*Managers build dependability through
accuracy; leaders build credibility through
authenticity.*

These seven powerful pauses run through all three remaining chapters of the book: Pause to Grow Personal Leadership; Pause to Grow Others; Pause to Grow Cultures of Innovation. They are the supporting practices to the meta-pause principle: "Step back to lead forward." As you progress through the next three chapters of the book, you will have the opportunity to apply these pauses in pragmatic ways to impact growth in all domains of leadership.

CHAPTER TWO

PAUSE TO GROW
PERSONAL LEADERSHIP

GROW THE WHOLE PERSON TO
GROW THE WHOLE LEADER

AN ANCIENT STORY FROM THE TALMUD illustrates our essential life journey. The story goes something like this: "Every blade of grass in all of creation has an angel standing over it, whispering three words of encouragement: Grow . . . Grow . . . Grow." Regardless of our individual belief systems—religious, scientific, or humanistic—most of us can relate to this core impulse in life: *Grow more, be more, contribute more, become more, serve more.* This is the essence of leadership . . . the implicit drive to grow, contribute, and create enduring value. Helping ourselves and others to pause to align with this primal growth impulse is the purpose of The Pause Principle.

Organizations tend to rise and fall in proportion to the personal growth and personal decline of its leaders. As the leader grows, so the enterprise goes. Personal leadership, growing as a whole person to grow as a whole leader, is fundamental to enduring leadership effectiveness and is essential to enduring organizational performance. We see this in our leadership development work, and research bears it out. "Self-awareness combined with interpersonal skills are convincing indicators of driving results and managing talent." One study showed:

> "results-at-all-costs" executives actually diminish the bottom line, especially over time, while self-aware leaders with strong interpersonal skills deliver better financial performance. . . . Conversely, an executive who is self-aware and good with staff will be better at working with clients and business partners, better at grasping and executing strategy, and better at delivering bottom line results. These mostly lower ego, trust-inspiring executives still hold the bar very high and demand strong performance. . . .

In the absence of our continuous growth as leaders, our chances of effectively dealing with complexity, and cultivating both innovation and sustainable growth are reduced. Our risk of hitting the VUCA wall individually and collectively greatly increases. Leaders expand or limit their enterprise and strategic growth in direct proportion to their personal leadership growth. As true as this may be, it is equally difficult for us as leaders to recognize the need in ourselves. When we are most frustrated with our teams or organizations, that is the time for us to step back to see how we could show up in new and different ways to optimize performance.

In a conversation with Daniel Vasella, M.D., chairman of Novartis, I asked him which competencies are most important to leadership. His response was, "While there are several business-relevant competencies including conceptual abilities, strategic agility, and results drive, self-reflection is the most important personality related aspect of leadership. Self-reflection helps you to discern precisely when to pause and when to act, as well as the underlying functional or dysfunctional reasons for doing so. Self-reflection gives you a self-regulating, self-monitoring process to understand how to lead and where your leadership is coming from." *Effective managers drive to results; leaders consciously and continuously reflect to gain new personal and strategic perspectives, then drive to value-creating contribution.*

James was the named CEO successor for a multibillion-dollar global manufacturing organization. He was strategic, quick, and innovative. But, the more he pushed his teams and colleagues to collaborate with him, the more they passively resisted. Without realizing it, he had taught them well to count on him for new strategies and innovative ideas. They knew their input wasn't really needed. James wanted collaboration, but his behavior modeled single-minded, unyielding, do-it-yourself brilliance. Who wanted to fight that battle? Fortunately, with coaching assistance, James paused. He stepped back to see his situation more clearly and to view his behavior and his position of power through the eyes of others. James also courageously paused to reflect on early life patterns that were counterproductive. Believe me, he was initially surprised by his discoveries. From this new perspective, he saw the incongruence of his behavior and what he said he wanted. He put himself in his teams' and colleagues' shoes and understood the natural hesitation of many people on his teams. To his credit, James became the change he wanted to see in his organization. James paused, and learned to become more self-aware through self-reflection, which began to unlock his potential, and many of the doorways of his team flew open, as well.

James wisely paused and took a new leadership approach. Research by Green Peak Partners in conjunction with Cornell University showed that strong people skills and self-awareness drive better strategic and financial results. In another study by Allan Church, W. Warner Burke Associates, researchers looked at managerial self-awareness, congruence between their own assessment of self and the assessments of others, and its connection to performance. "High Performers in this study were significantly more self-aware compared to Average Performers. . . . High Performers had a greater level of self-awareness and of assessing their own behavior in their workplace."

Pause Point:
Pause to Unlock Leadership Potential

Take a break. Sit down in your favorite spot. Turn on some light music if you like. Begin to reflect on your team highlights and lowlights. Think about the energizing and energy-draining aspects of your team. Consider how you show up with the team. Then, consider:

O What frustrates you most about your team?

O What would you like their new behaviors or outcomes to look like?

O What changes would need to happen to achieve this?

O What changes would need to happen *in you* to achieve this?

A global consumer products firm has an ambitious strategy to grow from $10 billion to $20 billion during the next five years. Growing principally through acquisitions over the past ten years, they have masterfully integrated numerous cultures to create a formidable organization. Realizing they needed to grow and invest in internal talent to get to their next growth goal, they did not just roll out a canned leadership development program for the masses. First, the top five executives, who were potential CEO successors, engaged in their own leadership development through our Chief Executive Institute. They completed comprehensive assessments. They worked intensely for three days with a team of our coaches and consultants. Then, they regularly received coaching over eighteen months. The organization saw how hard they dedicated themselves to the process. It became okay, even in their hard-charging, results-focused organization, to step back to understand themselves and step forward into leadership in new ways. The leaders of the organization paused, embodied the growth they wanted to see in others and in the organization. Subsequent leadership programs for the top people flowed easily. Leadership development was undeniably valued at the company. It was a clear, integral part of their success from a strategic and personal context. One of the top fifty executives commented, "If our most senior leaders are so personally engaged in their own development, I'm completely invested, too. We all need to grow, to build leadership capacity to meet the business growth that is coming."

OPENING UP THE LEADER WITHIN

Pausing for self-awareness is like unlocking the doors to a series of rooms. While reflective pause is the key to unlocking self-awareness, self-awareness in turn opens the doorways to authenticity, character, and purpose. Personal leadership growth is the ongoing process of being and becoming a more authentic leader. As leaders, we lead by virtue of who we are, so knowing who we are is the key to elevating our capacities and performance. In *Leadership from the Inside Out*, we explored extensively the principle of growing self-awareness and authenticity to foster leadership effectiveness. Since that initial writing, the research by Daniel Goleman, Jim Collins, Jack Zenger, and Joe Folkman and many others validates the pivotal relationship between self-awareness and leadership contribution.

Self-awareness is the most crucial developmental breakthrough for accelerating personal leadership growth and authenticity. Learning to pause to build self-awareness is a lifelong, evolving process. Why is pausing for self-awareness so critical to leaders? It is extremely valuable to know ourselves in order to leverage our potentialities:

- We need to know our strengths to assert them in the appropriate circumstances.
- We need to know our vulnerabilities, weaknesses, and distressing emotions, to check them and to prevent asserting them inappropriately and in non-value-creating ways.
- When we are not self-aware, people around us have a better sense of our strengths and weaknesses than we do, and we lose credibility.
- When we are self-aware, we are more in touch with reality; people trust and respect us more.

o When we are not fully aware of our strengths, we lose confidence, never really understanding or asserting our value.

o When we are not aware of our vulnerabilities, we rarely know when to step back and rely on others to fill or complete our gaps.

o When we are not self-aware, we are not listening. We have not listened to ourselves from the inside-out. We have not listened to the feedback of others from the outside-in. We are isolated and out of touch, inside and out.

o When we are self-aware, we can more fully and appropriately connect with others.

Throughout the ages, the phrase *nosce teipsum*, "Know thyself," is a classic theme. We discover it in the writings of Socrates, Ovid, Cicero, in the sayings of the Seven Sages of Greece, on the entrance to the Temple of Apollo, and in the early Christian texts. *Nosce teipsum* threads its way through history as one of the preeminent precepts in life. Contemporary thought leader Warren Bennis writes, "Letting the self emerge is the essential task of leaders." From Daniel Goleman we learned that self-awareness, self-management, and empathy are three abilities "that distinguish the best leaders from average." He asserts, "You put all those together in every act of leadership."

Why is self-awareness so tough to practice? As Bill George, former Medtronic CEO and bestselling author of *True North* explains,

Discovering our authentic leadership requires us to test ourselves, our values, and our beliefs through real-world experiences. This is not an easy process as we are constantly buffeted by the demands of the external world, the model of success that others hold for us, and our search to discover our truth. Because there is no map or direct path between where you are now and where you will go on your leadership journey, you need a compass to keep you focused on your True North and get back on track when you are pulled off by external forces or are at risk of being derailed.

St. Augustine reflected, "People travel to wonder at the height of mountains, at the huge waves of the sea, at the long courses of rivers, at the vast compass of the ocean, at the circular motion of the stars; and they pass by themselves without wondering." Knowing others is one indicator of emotional intelligence, but knowing ourselves is possibly the principal sign of wisdom. I think it is fair to say that leaders are somewhat obsessed with understanding and changing the world or the marketplace in which they operate, but only a few great leaders take the time to pause to understand and change themselves.

> *All real change begins with self-change; pause*
> *is a catalyst of self-change.*

Self-awareness nourishes authenticity, that irresistible quality of leaders who have more fully examined themselves and, as a result, more clearly see their gifts as well as their gaps. As Warren Bennis sees it, "To be authentic is literally to be your own author . . . to discover your own native energies and desires, and then to find your own way of acting on them." Vas Narasimhan, former president of Novartis Vaccines and now global head of development, told me, "When I am more aware, things slow down. In meetings, I hear more, think more, can observe and make better choices. It is a state of high performance, much like an athlete, who slows down the game and has a performance edge." Lao-Tzu fully captured the principle of self-awareness with the following: "He who knows others is wise. He who knows himself is enlightened."

Pause Point:
Self-Awareness 101

Take a pause. No rush. No hurry. Consider each question with as much objectivity and observation as possible. As you ponder each question, ask yourself, "How do I see this? How do others perceive this? How do I reconcile or integrate these views?"

◎ What are your strengths and gifts that create the most value?

o What are your vulnerabilities or development challenges?

o What insights have 360° assessments and other assessments given you regarding your strengths, gifts, and vulnerabilities?

o Where do these strengths come from? Who has influenced you the most? What situations have influenced you the most?

o What have the traumas and privileges of your life taught you?

o Recall the key peaks and valleys of your career and your life. What have you learned from them?

o Do people trust you? If they do, why? If they don't, why not?

o What would your dearest, most trusted friend or colleague say are your greatest strengths and your greatest weaknesses?

Expanding the Light
for a Broader View

In *The Social Animal*, David Brooks brilliantly synthesizes recent research in various scientific disciplines to explore how human beings understand themselves and see their world. He says, "We're able to function in a social world because we partially permeate each other's minds and understand—some people more and some people less." He notes, "Human beings understand others in themselves. . . ." He relates Alison Gopnik's insight that "adults have searchlight consciousness," while young children have "lantern consciousness" that "illuminates outward in all directions—a vivid panorama of awareness of everything."

What if we extended the circumference, the reach of light to expand our awareness? For self-awareness to be real, authentic, and grounded, it must be gained from both the inside-out and the outside-in. That is why it is important to pause to reflect intently on values, beliefs, patterns, characteristics, and personal history for an inside-out view, and just as important to pause to gain feedback, perspective, and insight from others for an outside-in view. This continuous, infinite, self-regulating loop of self-aware-ness from both the "I" (inside-out) and the "We" (outside-in) perspective helps us to come closer to authentic self-awareness. Since we can rarely fully govern external events, as leaders we are left principally to govern ourselves; pausing for self-awareness is authentic governance.

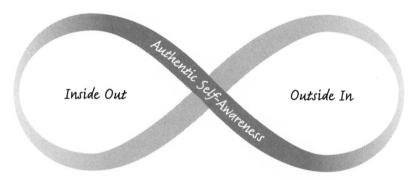

The Continuous Loop of Authentic Self-Awareness

WHAT IS THIS THING CALLED CHARACTER?

Managers require competency to drive results; leaders embody character to build a compelling, sustainable future.

Competencies get us to the doorway of leadership, but character is the key to unlocking the door of leadership. So what is this thing we call "char-acter"? It is our most authentic, unvarnished, non-spin-doctored self. It is the person and the leader who shows up—for better or worse—when no one is looking. Many leaders' characters would barely recognize their reputations if they met on the street! Character is the person others trust or mistrust from watching us in many, many situations. Character, in its highest state, is the leader who serves; in its lowest state, it is the leader who self-serves.

Character is that small, still voice that
sometimes is too loud for comfort in the
middle of the night, and sometimes is too faint
for influence in the heat of daily leadership.

Influenced by Emerson's essay, "Character," I define character as the quiet, reserved, value-creating force of the person, untouched by circumstances or external pressures. Character when aligned with action adds energy, value, service, and contribution to all it touches. Emerson goes on to say, "Character is higher than intellect." Einstein agreed. He pointed out, "Most people say intellect makes a great scientist. They are wrong, it is character."

Terry Bacon, a colleague and expert on power and influence, has conducted extensive research on the personal sources of power. His findings identify five personal power sources: knowledge, expressiveness, history, attractiveness, and character. Significant in his research, "character is the only source of power that can add to or subtract from every other source. You can be very knowledgeable, eloquent, attractive and have existing relationships with the people you are trying to influence, but if they perceive that your character is flawed, your power to lead and influence them will be greatly diminished." On the positive side of character, Bacon writes, "Being recognized as a person of character enhances your capacity to lead and influence others because they trust your intentions, are more confident in your leadership, and see you as a person worth emulating."

The Study of Character

One of the most comprehensive studies of character appears in *Character Strengths and Virtues* by Christopher Peterson and Martin Seligman. The research, done in coordination with the American Psychological Association and promoted by the Values in Action (VIA) Institute on Character, identifies twenty-four characteristic strengths in six factor areas. Terry Bacon includes results of this study in *The Elements of Power*. They are listed with some minor adaptations.

CHARACTER STRENGTHS FROM VALUES IN ACTION INSTITUTE

I. Wisdom and Knowledge
—Creativity
—Curiosity
—Judgment and Open-Mindedness
—Love of Learning
—Perspective

II. Courage
—Bravery
—Perseverance
—Honesty
—Zest/Vitality

III. Humanity
—Capacity to Love and Be Loved
—Kindness
—Social Intelligence

IV. Justice/Civic Strengths
—Teamwork
—Fairness
—Leadership

V. Temperance
—Forgiveness and Mercy
—Modesty and Humility
—Prudence
—Self-Control

VI. Transcendence
—Appreciation of Beauty
    and Excellence
—Gratitude
—Hope
—Humor
—Spirituality, Faith, Purpose

PAUSE POINT:
YOUR CHARACTER PATTERN

Pause for a moment on the list of twenty-four character strengths.

○ Which aspects of character are your top three strengths, the ones that others clearly see and appreciate?

○ Which aspects of character are your bottom three?

○ What do these aspects of character tell you about your current leadership development challenges?

○ What might you do more of, less of, or differently to elevate your character-driven leadership to the next level?

Too often, we idealize or vilify the character of others, which distracts us from facing our own character development. Pausing to get a clearer picture of our own character, strengths, and weaknesses is a crucial aspect of self-awareness and authenticity.

Two tools can help you measure your character profile:

1. The Values in Action Survey of Character provided by the Values in Action Institute (VIA) with its twenty-four character strengths in six factor areas as described previously.

2. The Character Foundation Assessment™ (CFA) from The Peirce Group, which measures twenty-two virtues along the five core values of Integrity, Vision/Creativity, Drive/Change, Responsibility and Influencing others. CFA was created based on the expertise of professionals in a variety of occupations to identify those virtues that are critical to success in business. Built into the CFA is a process that allows professionals to pause and reflect on these business critical virtues and to map a path forward for growing them to achieve their leadership development goals.

In *The Elements of Power*, Terry Bacon teamed up with Kim Ruyle and Evelyn Orr of Korn/Ferry International to map the VIA's classification of character with Korn/Ferry's Leadership Architect®. They estimated the degree of developmental difficulty for the six factors and twenty-four items. For the VIA factors, they found that the most difficult factors to develop were Humanity and Transcendence. Temperance, Wisdom and Knowledge, and Courage were easier factors to develop, and Justice/Civic Strengths was the easiest of all. On the VIA item level, the researchers identified Social Intelligence, Humor, Spirituality, and Perspective as the most difficult character strengths to develop, and Love of Learning, Perseverance, Modesty/Humility, and Zest/Vitality as the easiest.

While most of us wholeheartedly endorse character as critical to leadership, and most of us require it in the leaders we work for and seek out, few leaders consciously evaluate and seek to develop their own character. In the course of my career, I cannot recall a single leader asking, "Kevin, I have been struggling with my character. I think I need some work." We tend to complain about our eyesight and memory more than we criticize our own ethics and character. We acknowledge it as important, but we rarely, if ever, pause to genuinely examine it. Character and authenticity are very slippery subjects. We tend to expect these character qualities in others, require them in leaders, but rarely do we hold ourselves to the same standard.

Managers create processes and control mechanisms to regulate and enforce ethical behavior; leaders embody character to inspire ethical behavior in others.

Being Your Talk

Authenticity is the continual process of building self-awareness of our whole person—strengths and limitations. As a result of this more fully developed awareness, more often than not, the authentic person's beliefs, values, principles, and behaviors tend to line up. Commonly referred to as walking the talk, authenticity also means "being our talk" at a very deep level.

While we may be true and authentic to our current state of development, we are nearly always inauthentic to our potential state of development. As Shakespeare wrote in Hamlet, "We know what we are, but not what we may be." We appear to have an infinite ability to grow, to be, and to become more. If there is an endpoint to growing in authenticity, I certainly have not seen it. Growth is the ongoing process of stretching from our current state of authenticity to our next stage of authenticity.

A while ago, I was working with a senior team and CEO in the middle of a major crisis. Although the CEO needed to work on a few crucial growth areas, authenticity was not one of them. The COO, however, unknowingly was caught up in his image. He needed to stretch to a new level of authenticity. At a critical point in one of their interactions as the COO was placing an overly positive spin on mistakes made in an important decision, the CEO calmly and compassionately asked, "Bill, do you want to look good, or do you want to make a difference?" Bill fell silent. Of course he wanted to make a difference. He needed someone to shock him into a deeper state of authenticity and character. The character of the CEO penetrated the coping mechanism of the COO to reveal how he had to show up and serve in a new, more authentic way.

The Master and the Servant

A CEO of a major company told us that pausing helped her to see decision-making processes from a new perspective. She learned that pausing "strengthened her muscle of intention, instead of leaving choices and their impact to happenstance." This made her more conscious of the impact leaders have. Pausing to understand where her leadership is coming from—character or coping—has been a most valuable awareness. "It helps me to be clearer, to feel more confident in my choices and not feel unseated by other people's choices."

Character is the essence or core of the leader. Character is deeper and broader than any action or achievement; it springs from the essential nature of the person. Reflecting on this principle, Ralph Waldo Emerson wrote, "This is what we call character, a reserved force which acts directly as presence, and without means." Character works to transform and open up possibilities and potential. When we are leading from our character, we exude qualities of authenticity, purpose, openness, trust, courage, congruence, and compassion. We have the ability to transform circumstances, open up possibilities and create lasting value for ourselves and for others.

Coping, on the other hand, protects us and helps us get through challenging circumstances. In this sense, it has value, and if used sparingly and appropriately, will serve our needs. Coping works like a muscle. We need to use it at times, but if we overuse it, the muscle will collapse. Qualities of Coping include concern for image, safety, security, comfort, or control. The Coping leader may get results but also may exhibit undue defensiveness, fear, withdrawal, or a desire to win at all costs. He or she may exclude certain people and perceive mainly win/lose scenarios.

Both approaches to leadership—leading with Character and leading by Coping—can get results. Coping, in itself, is not bad and may be needed in certain situations. However, Character is a much better master, and Coping is a much better servant for leadership. For example, image may be a component of leadership, which can create influence and value when it is aligned with messages delivered from the leader's deeper values. Image may be used to manipulate messages in an attempt to compensate for a leader's insecurity, or lack of authenticity, and this may lead to devastating results.

Both Character and Coping are present in most leadership situations. However, we need to step back and ask ourselves, "Which one is my master and which one is my servant?" When we pause to consciously make Character the master of our leadership and Coping the servant, we lead forward with more value creation.

The Tiger, the Pig, the Ass, and the Nightingale

Is there anything more important than leaders leading in character, serving the needs of the broader enterprise and the communities in which they operate? We need leaders and want to develop leaders who place service to the enterprise and society above self-service, and there are many of them. Unfortunately, our society also is littered with the damage done by leaders with positional and competency power who lacked character power. Daily we read about another fallen leader in government, politics, business, and the nonprofit arena. *We do not merely suffer from a global financial crisis; we suffer from a global character crisis, which is fueling a global financial crisis because of self-focused decisions that are personal surrenders of character.* Leaders do not suddenly become bad people. It evolves over a "thousand tiny surrenders of self-respect to self-interest." Character is at the core of authenticity and emotional intelligence. The less self-aware the person, the less they feel remorse for what they have done or empathy for those they have hurt, and the more damage they are capable of perpetrating. On the one hand, we can get angry and self-righteous and say, "Those damn, unethical leaders, how could they do that?" Or, on the other, we can pause . . . recognize that we all have that potential to self-serve and engage our own commitment to making sure that we are acting in character. As Confucius advised, "When you meet a virtuous person, try to equal him. When you meet a person without virtue, look at your own shortcomings."

The battle between being self-serving and serving others is a continual human struggle. Ambrose Bierce wrote, "In each human heart are a tiger, a pig, an ass, and a nightingale. Diversity of character is due to their unequal activity!" So, the key question is, "How do we move from the ass to the nightingale more often?" If power indeed corrupts, how can we build *character immunity* before we face even more expanded power? The greatest threats are within us. Why worry about the fallen leaders we read about in the news feed? Let's focus on what threatens our souls. Blaming others for lack of ethics and character may distract us from taking the time to pause about the tough character-driven choices in our own lives. Become the character you want to see in others. George Bernard Shaw penned it this way, "Better keep yourself clean and bright; you are the window through which you must see the world." Channel the energy that could be lost in disgust, blame, and self-righteousness into "cleaning your window" through a continuous practice of pausing for character self-observation.

Where Is My Leadership Coming From?

Over the years, we have evolved and refined a way of observing our behavior using two modes to characterize our leading behavior: Leading in Character and Leading by Coping. Learning to self-observe, discern at any moment of leadership, and answer this question, "Where is my leadership coming from?" is crucial to moving into Character mode more often. The Character mode creates enduring energy, service, and value for others. The Coping mode tends to get results, but is focused more on self-service, self-survival, and rarely is a sustainable leadership approach. "Character is much easier kept than recovered," Thomas Paine advised us. It is crucial to understand in the heat of leadership how our actions or inactions are motivated by character or by coping.

LEADING BY COPING OR LEADING IN CHARACTER

Leading by Coping	Leading in Character
Self-serving	Other-serving
Depletes energy	Multiplies energy
Control	Trust
Image	Authenticity
Reactive	Proactive
Short term	Long term
Fear	Courage
Anger	Compassion
Winning at all costs	Serving at all costs
Silo-focused	System/Enterprise-focused
Destructive conflict	Constructive conflict
Distracted	Present
Uncomfortable demeanor	Calm demeanor
Overwhelmed by circumstances	Above the circumstances
Entrenched viewpoint	Humility, openness, learning
Closed-minded	Fair-minded
Critical/Judgmental	Humane/Tolerant
Dogmatic expertise	Wisdom
Rigidity	Transcendence

PAUSE POINT:
LEADING BY COPING

Imagine yourself in a stressed state. Too much to do, and way too little time. You feel the pressure building mentally, physically, and relationally. Now, one more major demand comes along, and you go into your coping mode.

○ Which of the coping behaviors listed in the table do you tend to go to? (Narrow it down to your two or three most common ones.)

○ How do you feel physically? What pressures or pains surface in your body? (Be specific.)

○ What related behaviors come up?

○ How does this impact self, relationships, and your work?

PAUSE POINT:
LEADING IN CHARACTER

Imagine yourself in a situation where you are at the top of your game, adding energy and contribution to everyone around you. Your values are present. Your strengths are operating, and even in a very challenging situation, you are calm and centered.

○ Which of the previous Character behaviors in the table tend to show up? (Again, choose two or three that are most common.)

○ How do you feel physically? How does your body feel differently from when you are in Coping mode? (Again, be specific.)

○ How does this impact self, relationships, and your work?

○ Can you discern the difference between the Coping and Character ways of leading?

○ How could you shift from Coping to Character more often?

Building self-awareness to move from coping to character in your leadership can be transformative for you and others. Practice it at home and migrate it to the office. Involve others in your practice. Leverage their outside-in feedback to keep yourself on track. Notice the energy benefit of character. Notice the energy depletion of coping. See your health improve, as well as your relationships at home and at work. See your leadership strengthen.

> *Character is power . . . the power to create*
> *rather than destroy; the power to energize*
> *rather than deflate; the power to serve others*
> *rather than merely serving self.*

Leveraging the power of character is a practice we can consciously choose. The choice is ours in every moment of life and leadership. As Charles de

Gaulle said, "Faced with crisis, the man of character falls back upon himself." Possibly the most character-driven U.S. President, Abraham Lincoln, understood the leadership challenge well. "Nearly all men can stand adversity, but if you want to test a man's character, give him power." Pause to practice character; ready yourself for the next moment of personal or professional power.

WAITING FOR OUR SPIRITS
TO CATCH UP

My good friend, consultant, and bestselling author, Richard Leider, spends a month each year with a group of leaders trekking with the Hadza, a hunter-gatherer tribe, in the Lake Eyasi region south of the famed Serengeti Plains of Tanzania, East Africa. After he returned from one of these experiences, he told me a wonderful story:

> The African sun had sucked most of the oxygen out of the air with its all-consuming fire. Everything was a combination of heat, dust, and sweat. Focused on our goal, we needed to get to the next landmark by sunset. This was achievable but a challenge. Suddenly and unexpectedly our Hadza guides sat down, unwilling to move. A bit surprised and upset, I went to the group and asked, "What are you doing? We have to go." Unfazed, the group leader spoke with calm reserve, "Sir, we have to stay here so our spirits can catch up to our bodies. We have been going too fast. Now, we have to pause and wait."

How often are we going too fast? Our pace outstripping the slower tempo of the deepest, most important part of ourselves—our values, beliefs, principles, and deepest character—from joining us or "keeping up"?

PAUSE FOR OUR
DEEPEST VALUES

A while ago, I was coaching one of the most brilliant, driven, and creative global CEOs I have ever worked with. He was exceptional on nearly every level. He was strategic, innovative, and passionate. He was also one of the fiercest leaders I have ever encountered. Without notice, he could grow impatient and take people apart. As a result, people were careful and hesitant around him. But carefulness and hesitation made him more impatient, increasing his tension and frustration, as well as the likelihood of his acting even more fiercely. He needed a pause to unravel this knot. Working together over several months, we were able to see a clearer, more complete picture. In one very poignant session, I pressed him for about an hour on, "What is he really about? Is getting results and driving people his real thing? What does he want to be remembered for? Where is all this passion and drive coming from? What does he care about most?" He got very quiet, took a deep, deep pause . . . and said, "What I care most deeply about is love. It is the one thing I most want my life to be about. Love." I nearly fell out of my chair. Love! This was the last thing I expected to hear. To challenge him, I responded, "Love? Would people describe you as loving?" He thought for a moment and said, "Probably not at work, but my family would say that I am very loving, and passionately committed to them." He had fallen into a classic leadership trap. In his drive forward, he had left behind one of his greatest, most essential values: deep human connection. To his credit, over time, he courageously stepped back to retrieve and integrate this powerful attribute into his fuller, more human, leadership repertoire.

Deborah Dunsire, M.D., CEO of Millennium Pharmaceutical: The Takeda Oncology Company, is very clear about the importance of pausing with her teams, especially in crises situations. She told us, "It's important to make sure that your organization's values are on the table early on. That way you don't waste time." To illustrate, she told us about a situation in which a single-digit number of vials of a drug outside the United States were found to have single, scarcely visible particles in them. She and her team were going to have to determine whether or not this was a voluntary recall situation within the United States, where there had been no complaints. She told me, "Our values are clear: Patient safety is number one. Quality and Compliance are number two. Corporate reputation is number three. The cost or amount of money lost is not a consideration on product safety issues. Our job is to keep the patient safe and continue their access to effective therapies. There is no compromising on that. These values drive how we make these decisions." From that position, everyone gathered around the table, and they took their time walking through the situation together, asking questions, listening, pausing to seek information, and not rushing to judgment. She probed, "What is your expert opinion? Help me understand how you got there. Tell me how you came to this concern." Deborah said, "Stepping through it is grounding. Everyone has the same fact base. It encourages synthesis and establishes priorities." *Managers pride themselves on rapid decision making, while leaders know the value of slowing down to incorporate values and purpose into more grounded and thoughtful decision making.*

Pausing to find our deepest values and bringing them to all our domains of leadership may be the most crucial aspect of our development as whole leaders. Warren Bennis counsels us that "leaders remind people what is important." However, to remind people, we have to know what is important in our hearts and guts. What do we stand for as leaders? What do we know for sure? What has our particular life with all its privileges and traumas taught us about what is important? To gain self-awareness, we need to pause and ground ourselves in the deepest value-creating regions within our character. Albert Einstein had it right when he said, "Try not to become a man of success, become a man of value."

PAUSE POINT:
CLARIFY VALUES

Step back now. Take a deep breath. Set aside a moment to pause and consider these questions. Remember, questions are the language of pause. Consider your ideals and your aspirations . . . what you hold most important:

o What do you care most about?

o What energizes you most?

o What cause would you dedicate yourself to? Why?

o Where and when do you need to slow down to let your values catch up?

o What losses in life have impacted you the most? What did you learn about what is most precious?

o What bothers you in the world that you would most like to change? Why?

Purpose: The Transformative Force of Leadership

Pausing for Purpose is the essential transformational force of leadership. Purpose elevates leaders to go from self to service and compels leaders to move from success to significance. Purpose nourishes the heart and the soul of leadership.

> *The art of leadership involves elevating souls*
> *beyond the dust of daily living; purpose*
> *shakes the dust off of the everyday fabric*
> *of management, revealing the interwoven*
> *patterns of leadership meaning and service.*

Pausing for Purpose is one of the leader's most important practices to prepare for value-creating, enduring performance.

Steve Jobs is deservedly regarded as the business and cultural icon of innovation. I view him as an icon of purpose. What drove his innovation? What was the originating force from which he created? His interviews with his biographer Walter Isaacson and reports by others who knew him reveal how much he was driven by beauty and aesthetics. His Zen-inspired drive for the profoundly simple and the profoundly elegant were ever-present. He was an artist at heart, sculpting a bridge between technology and humanity. Each creation—product, service, or innovation—had an intimate human connection that created a passionately committed user experience. Who else but an artist could create devices that were so human-centric and human serving? Although Apple cofounder Steve Wozniak may be a kinder, gentler, more technologically talented human being, he didn't have the same passion for aesthetics. Jobs was a much tougher person with less technological strength, but his innovations embodied an aesthetic value that translated to an emotional connection for the customer that very few understood and believed was possible. Steve Jobs expected everything and everyone (for better or worse) to measure up to his extreme, sometimes impossible standards. His purposeful drive to "put a dent in the universe" was fueled by the "artist's ideal" for beauty, elegance, and essence. Jobs operated at the intersection of humanity and technology, art and science. His vision, expectations, discrimination, and sense of beauty leveraged technology to serve humanity. He changed the world through his passion and purpose.

Jobs's purpose endured throughout great personal trauma. In the intensive care unit toward the end of his life, he asked for a notepad. He drew devices to hold the iPad on a hospital bed; he redesigned fluid monitors and X-ray equipment. Jobs's purpose, his drive to make a value-creating difference, was breaking through, seeking expression to the very end.

> *While we all die to some degree in the middle*
> *of our story, the underlying meaning and plot*
> *of our life story—our purpose—lives on.*

Getting to the Heart of Purpose

Laura Karet recently became CEO of Giant Eagle, a four-generation $10-billion grocery retailer in the northeastern United States. Giant Eagle has a long, successful history, a well-developed values system that includes a strong sense of community, and its previous CEO, David Shapira, was renowned for his creative, innovative, and visionary prowess. The company has a very rich, multigeneration family legacy. Laura had planned a career outside the family business but eventually agreed to return home after successful opportunities with Procter & Gamble and Sara Lee Corporation.

Laura wants to take the organization to the next level, leveraging her marketing, branding, and consumer products background from her pre–Giant Eagle career. She astutely realized that this transition was a great opportunity to pause and reflect to gain some insight on what is working well and what isn't. She realized that those qualities that make her different from her father are perhaps most valuable. She thought, "What do we want to hold onto that is part of the legacy, and what can I bring that is new, that will help grow the company, and make a contribution?" She said, "You can't afford to use only old lenses; you have to look with a fresh lens."

Laura explained that the nature of the grocery business can be very reactionary. People are accustomed to dealing with a wide range of incidents that can happen at any given moment. This works well in many aspects of the business, but Laura was determined to bring more disciplined strategizing, teaming, and talent development processes to Giant Eagle. She wanted to develop more long-term thinking and planning. It took a strong resolve, patience, and tenacity, but she used the discipline of pausing to ask probing questions when she took her senior team off-site to confront important issues, to become more open and collaborative, to get them thinking long range . . . to deal with what is important. During our coaching, Laura learned to pause to listen more deeply and to absorb information, to not react, but to be more thoughtful and responsive. She is working toward integrating this dynamic into the culture of the 35,000 Team Member (employee) organization.

However, what Laura became most inspired to do was to invigorate the purpose and mission of the organization and herself with "a living value" that was inspired by her yoga practice. Laura, like many other yoga practitioners, ends each yoga session with the word *Namaste*. When used like this, it is an expression of honor and respect for yourself, your teachers, and your community. This struck a chord for Laura. She believes in her heart that all human beings deserve respect. Laura has made the connection to "the gift of leadership as an avenue to change the world in sometimes small and sometimes big ways." She has embodied this value, "respect for all people" in the culture of the company and extends it to everyone it serves—employees, customers, suppliers, the extended communities of all its stores. This meaningful intersection has given Laura a stronger, even more authentic connection to a place from which to lead that is energizing for Team Members, customers, and herself.

Through her dedication, self-inquiry, and pause, Laura now has a place to carry on the family legacy and to make her own mark. Taking the time to clarify purpose, stepping back to step forward with renewed strength and conviction is one of the most crucial things we can do as leaders of our organizations . . . and as leaders in life.

The pathway to purpose is charted with the compass of pause. Having a sense of purpose is having a sense of self, "a course to plot, a destination to hope for," Bryant McGill wrote. Just as explorers need to stop, pause, and establish their bearing periodically to stay on track, leaders need to step back on a regular basis, not just in crisis situations, to recalibrate their direction via mission and purpose.

Stepping back to clarify organizational mission, although challenging, is often easier than clarifying personal mission and personal core purpose. To get to the heart of our individual core purpose takes regular doses of pause. Accessing and maintaining a clear core purpose benefits the leader and the enterprise. Clarifying purpose:

- Strengthens self-awareness and the core contribution we bring
- Bolsters the power of our passionate voice; people see what we stand for
- Reinforces that service is the key to purposeful leadership; allows us to see our value-creating, value-serving influence
- Allows us to understand when to step into situations with full force and when to step back for others to show up
- Provides a frame of reference for when we need to assert, without inhibition, our strengths in service of purpose, and when a leader needs to pause to clarify purpose, impact, and learning

Helping leaders to define and clarify core purpose may be both the most overlooked and important process for accelerating leadership development. Without purpose, leaders are merely a sophisticated combination of competencies, like a pile of beautiful dry wood awaiting a spark to ignite its latent energy.

What Is This Thing Called Core Purpose?

Leaders rarely fail due to lack of talent; success or failure is mainly the domain of character, values, and purpose. Core Purpose is the high-performance intersection of a leader's core strengths in service of his or her core values. Core Purpose is the sweet spot of leadership, where the whole person is present, self-aware, and bringing his or her talents to bear by serving what is most important. Imagine the times in your life when you were using the best parts of yourself. You were engaged in and contributing to what you are most passionate about. This is Core Purpose. Take a moment to remember the times your energy was high, your sense of contribution clear, and your value-creating impact was great. This is Core Purpose. *Core Purpose is the soul on fire impacting positive change.* It is the ultimate convergence of the best of "I" and the best of "We" leadership. The strengths of the "I" are actively engaged in serving the needs of something greater—the larger "We." We contribute to something bigger than ourselves through our unique combination of strengths, knowledge, expertise, and competencies. Purpose inspires a leader's passion, awakens a leader's energy, and that force of energy impacts the world. Howard Schultz, CEO of Starbucks and author of *Onward*, says that at the core for him is his deep love for the company and a sense of responsibility to its people. "People want to be part of something larger than themselves *if they believe in it.* There has to be an emotional connection that is based on truth and authenticity, and, obviously, trust."

Is This All
There Is?

The classic midlife crisis is the gut-wrenching realization that well-earned achievement and competence in the absence of meaningful contribution is not enough. It is the anxiety-provoking realization that our strengths have not been in service of something bigger. As a result, we wonder, "Is this it? Is this all there is?" *Our deepest heart's desire, our greatest happiness comes from fully spending ourselves and our gifts in service to something bigger and more important.*

Most leaders understand the value of connecting a group of people to a bigger, external aspiration—a project, strategy, or goal. However, our ability to inspire others to a higher purpose begins somewhere within us. To inspire others, we must self-inspire first; we must ignite and crystallize our own purpose by clarifying our core talents, core values, and core contribution.

Core Purpose is a lifelong journey of pausing, reflecting, and fostering clarity. While the core remains the same, the clarity and usefulness of it grows through practice. For years, I have been crafting my Core Purpose statement. In the beginning, it was a long, complex statement of mission, aspiration, and contribution. It held a lot of principles, a lot of passion, but it was cumbersome and wordy. It read more like words on a plaque than a living, breathing guide. I wanted to breathe some life into it. Over time, with sufficient reflection, I distilled it from several words—"Using presence, passion, and purpose to catalyze growth"—to two words, "Catalyze growth," to one essential word . . . "Growth." Growth is the defining theme, the thing that I aspire to in myself and for others. Growth is why I write books. It influences whom I select as friends and colleagues, what I read, where I vacation, and certainly my life's work, from which I have no desire to retire. It is concurrently the aspiration and underlying plot of my story, my life. What is yours?

Pause Point:
Distilling Your Purpose

Go to your favorite spot. Find your best way to get relaxed. Reflect on the most energizing, fulfilling times of your life. Then, ask yourself:

○ Which of your strengths are showing up? What are you contributing?

○ What impact is this having on others? What are you serving?

○ What are others saying about your strengths, values, and contributions?

○ What is the passionate contribution you are making?

○ What themes do you observe threading through your life? What are the themes of your strengths? What are the themes of your values?

○ If you were the main character in a novel, what is the plot of your story, and what is the underlying theme that drives you? What value are you adding to the story? How are your talents and strengths and your contributions impacting others?

○ What is the one thing—the thing that you must contribute or that you aspire to contribute—from which you do not want to retire?

Return to this Pause Point many times. Make it your practice to clearly distill the themes of Core Purpose.

Since the recurring theme or organizing principle of my passion and my life is growth, when my competencies are contributing to growth, then my energies are high and my talents are connected to something much more important and larger than myself. This thread of purpose, as I think of it, can be traced back throughout our lives to connect all the relevant experiences and contributions into a tapestry of meaning. In my case, my family history, spiritual practices, educational choices, key relationships, life crises, and my leadership development career are all organized around this consistent, enduring theme of growth. When I wander away from this theme, not attending to my growth or the growth of others in personal or professional domains, my energy falls, struggle increases, and contribution diminishes. If we are paying attention, our alignment or lack of alignment with Core Purpose can give us moment-to-moment, breath-to-breath, real-time feedback on our authentic leadership performance.

PAUSE POINT:
CHECKING YOUR ALIGNMENT TO CORE PURPOSE

Some pause practices to align with Core Purpose and to strengthen our leadership impact include:

- Pause to observe when your energy is high or when you are increasing energy in others. During these times, pause to witness the strengths and values that are operating.

- Pause to observe when your energy or the energy of others drops to signal that you are out of synch with Core Purpose. Notice if your strengths are being overused or your values are not being expressed and embodied in your actions.

- Once you have identified your key themes of Core Purpose, pause to evaluate your congruence with it on a scale of 1 to 10.

Alignment with current position   = _____

Alignment with current team   = _____

Alignment with previous positions   = _____

Alignment with family or spouse   = _____

Alignment with friends   = _____

Alignment with community   = _____

Alignment with self *   = _____

o Pause to notice when your leadership voice is stronger and more compelling. Pay attention to those value-creating moments when your talents and passion are supporting your leadership conviction, when your full person is behind the act of leadership.

o Step back periodically to edit, refine, and update your Core Purpose statement as you deepen your understanding and your own growth.

o Pause during meetings to ask yourself, "Am I in alignment or out of alignment with Core Purpose at this moment?"

Take the time to step back to get to know your purpose; doing so will expand leadership possibilities. Alfred Whitehead put it this way: "Our minds are finite, and yet even in these circumstances of finitude we are surrounded by possibilities that are infinite, and the purpose of life is to grasp as much as we can out of that infinitude."

* This is the toughest one to face objectively. Reflect on this question: "How much am I applying this Core Purpose to myself?"

RESTORATIVE PAUSE: POWER NAP ANYONE?

As leaders, we do too much and rest too little. Restorative pause through meditation, exercise, power naps, and enough sleep are crucial. With 24/7 connectivity, global travel, jet lag, inadequate diet, irregular exercise, and insufficient vacations, it is a wonder that leaders survive. Behind the scenes, outside of the boardroom, the view is not so pretty. Health issues, relationship stress, and exhaustion are common. What do you do to restore yourself daily? Weekly? Quarterly?

Even walking 30 minutes a day, five times a week can be transformative, stimulating brain-derived neurotrophic factor (BDNF), a molecule that nurtures the creation of new neurons and synapses that support learning. Scientists at the University of Illinois-Champaign, have shown that exercise increases the gray matter in the brain that processes new information and sends it to permanent storage in the prefrontal cortex. Pausing to exercise can literally improve your learning and brain function.

Power naps can be amazing restorative pauses for many. Nike and a host of Silicon Valley companies, like Google, provide "nap rooms" for employees. In our office, we call it a "health room." I go there, turn off the lights, and return a new person in 15 to 20 minutes. In a 2010 study, Mathew Walker and colleagues at University of California–Berkeley found that a nap not only restored brain power but raised it. "In people who stayed awake, there was a deterioration in their memory capacity, but a nap restored that capacity to levels even higher than before the nap."

If you took some time each day to work in more restorative pause, what would you do? When will you begin?

Transcendental Pause: Getting to Essence

A large business school asked me to facilitate their collaborative process of crafting a consolidated viewpoint on leadership. Flattered, I accepted eagerly. But, after being in the room for only an hour with seventy professors and almost as many dueling egos asserting their "I have the best research" attitudes, I was ready to call it a day and fly home. I didn't. My curiosity won out, and surprisingly, after a couple of hours, we had agreed on a pretty solid, comprehensive model. There was a feeling of satisfaction and resolve in the room. I thought we were done, when a quiet professor stood up and said, "This leadership model with all its competencies—vision, strategy, learning, collaboration, team effectiveness, character, emotional intelligence—is all well and good, but we have ignored the essence of leadership." As you can imagine after working for a few hours and feeling like they were done, many of his cohorts were a little annoyed. A collection of groans and glares zeroed in on him. I was curious, as were others, and I said, "What did we leave out? And, from your colleagues' reactions, this had better be good." He said, "The essence of leadership is transcendence." More groans, glares, and a muttering fluttered through the room in response. "Transcendence. What is he thinking?" Our rebel was unshaken, and he continued, "Managers improve what is. Managers enhance what is. Managers move forward what is. Leaders, on the other hand, move beyond or transcend what is. So, where is *transcendence* in our model?" The room went quiet as everyone absorbed his insight, which captured the essence of leadership. *Managers build credibility through efficient, productive transaction; whereas leaders create the future through game-changing transcendence.*

Leadership, by its very nature transcends what is. To lead a great strategy, we must go beyond what is. To foster innovation, we must transcend current reality. To go to the next level of personal leadership, we need to go beyond our current state of growth.

> *The nature of leadership is constant boundary-breaking, ever-changing, mind-bending, heart-expanding, character-stretching, purpose-aspiring transcendence.*

For many, transcendence may seem a lofty, other-worldly, rarely attainable goal. To me, transcendence is everywhere; it is ever-present and ever-pragmatic, too. As leaders of organizations and as leaders in life, we are continually challenged to see strategy, relationships, and life in new and different ways. How often have you had an unexpected breakthrough while in the shower, during a run, or while taking a walk? This is the experience of transcendence. When have you been so deep in thought that external noise and distractions fade totally into the background? Transcendence. When have you stepped back to see new dimensions of yourself—strengths and limitations—from a new perspective? Transcendence. When have you had an innovative breakthrough with the corresponding *Aha!* moment? That is transcendence.

That moment, that flash of insight usually arises from a deeper, longer process of incubating ideas. Albert Einstein's theory of relativity had an incubation period of ten years. The beautiful array of fonts that accompanied the first Macintosh, which we take for granted on our computers today emerged from Steve Jobs's incubation of what he learned from studying calligraphy at Reed College. As scientists across disciplines have discovered, we have different ways of thinking, different cognitive processes going on in different areas of our mind, and some of them, or more accurately most of them, are currently hidden in our unconscious, waiting for a deep enough pause to make them accessible, to put together patterns based on what we have stored in our memory.

Change or Be Changed

Imagine a leader or an organization that somehow manages to maintain the status quo over many years. . . . It is only a matter of time before the tsunami of change washes over the firm. As leaders we must be tsunamis of purposeful change, be the accelerators of continual transcendence. If we do not, if we are not the initiators of change, the initiators of transcendence, the marketplace will force change upon us.

> *The one constant in leadership is,*
> *change or be changed; transcend or be*
> *forced to transcend.*

In the last chapter of this book, "Pause to Grow Cultures of Innovation," we discuss organizational transcendence. This final chapter provides tools and resources to let the future emerge, to transcend the present, and to innovate value-creating contributions.

Deep Transcendental Pause—Pause with a Big P

In this chapter we have been exploring personal transcendence. This is a pause in itself. We have been pausing to grow to the next level of leadership through self-awareness, character, and purpose. These are crucial and fundamental pause practices to "go beyond," to transcend, and to pause with a small p. However, there is another state of transcendence, another state of pause, a more powerful one: Pause with a big *P*.

This capital Pause is a state of life that goes to our deepest essence, our innermost reality as a human being and as a leader. The sages throughout history have had many names for this: *transcendental consciousness, pure consciousness, the absolute, the still point, silence itself, the soul,* or *essence.* Physicists have speculated about it as part of the unified field theory, a unifying web of life connecting everything and existing everywhere. Practitioners of meditation call it *consciousness with no thought, a state of being, mindfulness,* or *deep peace.* Researchers have described it as a unique mind-body state where brain activity is very coherent and the body is metabolically more than two times as rested as when in deep sleep. To date, more than 600 research studies have been conducted on one meditation technique, Transcendental Meditation (TM), at more than 250 universities and medical schools in thirty-three countries. Findings range from improved brain functioning to improved health, reduced blood pressure, increased creativity, improved learning ability, and higher levels of self-actualization. Other meditative practices have produced noteworthy research as well. Many meditators around the world practice mindfulness meditation to manage stress, high blood pressure, chronic pain, insomnia, anxiety, and depression as well as to increase focus.

Jon Kabat-Zinn, scientist and founder of the Center for Mindfulness in Medicine, Health Care, and Society at the University of Massachusetts Medical School as well as the renowned Mindfulness-Based Stress Reduction program, has pioneered the integration of mindfulness in our culture for more than three decades. In conversation with Bill Moyers about meditation during the PBS *Healing of the Mind* series, Kabat-Zinn said:

> We do know that human beings have a capacity for awareness and self-observation. People have learned how to step back from their own thought processes to the point where they're no longer making strong unconscious identifications with "I, me, and mine." When something comes up and you can say, "Wow, I haven't seen this one before," it's an example of becoming the scientist of one's own mind/body connection. Being a scientist of your own mind/body connection doesn't mean you have to control it. . . . What it means is that you'll live more intelligently.

You'll make decisions that are more apt to bring you in touch with the way things work for you in the world.

Abraham Maslow referred to transcendent pause as our "peak experiences," characterized by deep peace and fulfillment. Athletes call it "the zone," mind fully awake and at peace, body dynamically at a peak performance with the event witnessed, as if in slow motion. Psychologist Mihaly Csikszentmihalyi calls this optimal experience "flow." Otto Scharmer, Peter Senge, and others call this deep Pause "presencing." It is the bottom of the U in Scharmer's Theory U, the source of innovation, incubating, and giving rise to future possibilities.

But, what do leaders call it? Where is this deepest state of Pause in the leadership lexicon? For leaders the nomenclature may be less important than the more important knowledge that it is accessible and available to enhance the quality of our leadership performance. As leaders, this state of transcendence can refresh us, bring us to a deeper state of synthesis and creativity by crystalizing our thinking, building our resilience, increasing our presence, bringing peace to chaos and understanding to unpredictability. This state also brings us a deeper state of identity than our external, successful selves, and guides us to a more essential level of wisdom-led eldership. Jon Kabat-Zinn offers this perspective on transcendence, the "interior landscape":

> to explore the interior landscape of the mind and body, the realm of what Chinese Taoism and Chan masters called non-doing, the domain of true meditation, in which it looks as though nothing or nothing much is happening or being done, but at the same time, nothing important is being left undone, and as a consequence, that mysterious energy of an open, aware non-doing can manifest in the world of doing in remarkable ways.

Too often, managers are Human Doers using energy and action to spend themselves in the pursuit of goals, whereas leaders aspire to be full Human Beings seeking the renewal of transcendence to re-create themselves and others in pursuit of service-fueled purpose.

It was Roger Sperry, Nobel Prize winner in 1981, whose research demonstrated that our divided brain with two hemispheres was more creative, artistic and intuitive on the right and more analytical and logical on the left. However, more modern cross-disciplinary science shows that we do not have a split brain, but a whole brain with "intelligent memory" that works in concert, intuition and analysis together. Dr. Erik Kandel contributed to a breakthrough article along with Brenda Milner and Larry Squire, "Cognitive Neuroscience and the Study of Memory," in the journal *Neuron*, which explained this new model, and Kandel won the Nobel Prize in 2000 for his contribution. In "How Aha! Really Happens," William Duggan references this groundbreaking work and explains, "Whether it's working on a familiar formula or a new idea, intelligent memory combines analysis and intuition as learning and recall." The flash of insight or "Aha!" experience we sometimes feel is a result of the "combining of different pieces into a new pattern."

With awareness of this new model, research with functional MRIs, and cross-disciplinary approaches to studying the brain and the mind, we are learning about the conscious mind and the unconscious mind. In fact, Timothy Wilson, professor of psychology at University of Virginia, researcher, and author of *Strangers to Ourselves: Discovering the Adaptive Unconscious,* said on the "Consciousness" episode of the *Charlie Rose Brain Series* in 2011 that we learn much about the unconscious by studying the conscious mind, and the reverse is true, too. He, Erik Kandel, Daniel Gilbert, Patricia Churchland, and others participating in the discussion agreed that when one part of the brain quiets or is less active, the other part can become more active. In his book, *A Whole New Mind,* Dan Pink points out that Betty Edwards, the Harvard University art instructor famous for her course and book, *Drawing on the Right Side of the Brain,* insisted that the difficulty for many people when trying to draw is "Seeing . . . and the secret to seeing—really seeing—was quieting the bossy know-it-all left brain so the mellower right brain could do its magic." In *Strangers to Ourselves,* Wilson says, "The mind operates most efficiently by relegating a good deal of high-level, sophisticated thinking to the unconscious, just as a modern jumbo jetliner is able to fly on automatic pilot with little or no input from the human, 'conscious,' pilot." Deep pause is the activating mechanism to make the entire range of consciousness useful; it allows more of the organizing, pattern detecting, and creative power of the brain to be activated.

We see this state of transcendence in great leaders, such as Nelson Mandela and Mahatma Gandhi. When they are so deeply established in this state, no external event can shake them. Where do you go when times get really tough for you as a leader? Do you go to a loved one, a trusted advisor or friend? Do you try to work it out while you exercise? These options are helpful, but where do you go when you need the deepest counsel and solace? Prayer? Meditation? Music? Learning to go deeper and deeper into our Pause to counter balance our everything-coming-at-us-at-once life has never been more critical. Chunyi Lin, international qigong master, creator of Spring Forest Qigong, and one of the most enlightened people I know, shared with me, "It is in the deepest silence that we have the greatest power. Deep silence connects us to universal power, knowledge and creative potential. Go to the deepest level of self to access transformation in all parts of your life. Lead your self, lead others and lead your life from the depths of silence." As the British poet Lord Byron wrote, "The soul must pause to breathe."

PAUSE POINT:
DEEP PAUSE

Go to your favorite quiet place. Turn on some soft music, if you like. Or, say a prayer if that fits your beliefs and practice. Notice your breathing, in and out. Let your mind be easy and relaxed. You have nowhere to go, nothing to do. Breathe …in and out. Observe your thoughts like clouds passing in the sky. Watch them come and watch them go. Breathe . . . in and out. Let your mind sink deeper into itself, relaxed and expanded with no expectations, no time commitment, and nowhere to be but here. Relax and be. If you feel some anxiety or fears, watch them like a scene in a movie. See them come; see them go. If big worries enter, notice the related tension in your body and sit with it until it releases and your mind and emotions settle again. Breathe in and out. Relax and observe. Experience the profound rest, silence, and peace. Be. Doing comes later. For now, just be. After 10 to 20 minutes … take your time … very slowly open your eyes.

Move your fingers, turn your head, pull your shoulders back and down, maybe stretch a bit. Take some deep breaths.

○ What did you notice?

○ Were you able to observe the cycles of thoughts, anxiety, depth, rest?

○ How do you feel now?

○ Did you have some very deep, restful moments?

○ Would it be possible to pause more often like this to relax and reconnect more deeply?

○ What would be the benefits to you to learn to take deep pause? Would it strengthen you as a person? Would it strengthen you as a leader?

Turning this kind of deep pause into a practice is key for gathering its generative impact. The more often and regularly you practice, the more you will experience the benefit. When something knocks you off center, you will return to your centered, grounded place more quickly. Although meditation is a great way to connect deeply, there are many other ways: inspirational reading; listening to or playing music; walking in nature; practicing tai chi, qigong, or yoga; praying. The idea is to pay attention, tune in, or be aware in the present moment. The key is finding your own best ways to pause deeply and to practice them regularly to strengthen your personal leadership. Pause deeply to lead powerfully.

Step Back to Lead Forward: Seven Pause Practices to Grow Personal Leadership

Pause to Grow Personal Leadership Practice 1: Be On-Purpose

Purpose is the high-performing, value-creating intersection of core talents and core values. Pausing to be on-purpose gives context, meaning, and clear aspiration to our personal leadership growth. Take the time to sort out your core talents, core values, and the meaningful difference you want to make. *Managers control systems and processes to produce results; leaders foster meaning and purpose to achieve transformative growth.*

Pause to Grow Personal Leadership Practice 2: Question and Listen

Use powerful questions and deep listening to accelerate self-awareness and self-knowledge. Deep questions and deep listening are the two primary tools for reflection, insight, growth, and powerful action. Take some time daily to consider deeper, penetrating questions about your life and desired future. Then, step back and listen to your inner dialogue, resistance, and insight. As things become clear, consider another round of questions, listening, and insight. Learn ways to slow down to listen deeply to the quiet stirrings in your soul, accessed through profound questions and deep pause.

Pause to Grow Personal Leadership Practice 3: Risk Experimentation

Risk "trying on" new behaviors. Consider showing more appreciation, celebrating successes, or acknowledging contributions you previously took for granted. What do you notice in yourself? In others? Risk showing a deeper, more authentic side of yourself. Experiment . . . learn . . . adjust . . . experiment again. Find new ways of being and behaving that serve others, create value, and align with your purpose. Stretch yourself into new behaviors and new assignments, extracting the continuous learning along the way.

Pause to Grow Personal Leadership Practice 4: Reflect and Synthesize

Take 10 to 15 minutes daily at the beginning or end of the day to sort through events and issues, your feelings and concerns of the day. What happened? What went well? What did not go well? What have you learned? When facing very complex or difficult situations, take more time. Get input from others. Sort out different ways of looking at the challenge. "If the person I admire the most were faced with this situation, what would he or she do? If I completely lived my purpose, what would I do?" Challenge yourself daily to reflect and synthesize to foster heightened clarity.

Pause to Grow Personal Leadership Practice 5: Consider Inside-Out and Outside-In Dynamics

The most complete picture of our deepest selves is revealed in both the outer connection and community we achieve with others as well as in the inner com-

munion we achieve through introspection. Step back to consider the gaps and overlaps between how you perceive yourself and how others perceive you. Do you see strengths they do not? Do they see weaknesses in you that you do not? Pause to reconcile the similarities and differences between your self-awareness and the perceptions of others. Self-awareness, the keystone of authentic leadership, requires being open to sorting out these perceptions. Get an annual 360° and genuinely own your strengths and development challenges. Pause to create a comprehensive development plan.

Pause to Grow Personal Leadership Practice 6: Foster Generativity

Usually generativity is a concept reserved for preparing the next generation. However, it also applies to us. How are you being generative to yourself? Helping yourself to get ready for a new future, for the "next generation" of you? Reflect generatively by asking yourself, What is the next stage of my career contribution? What is the next stage of my personal and family life? What do I want to be remembered for? If it were your eightieth birthday, what do you hope people are thanking you for? Be generative to yourself; it can inspire personal transformation and personal reinvention.

Pause to Grow Personal Leadership Practice 7: Be Authentic

There is no better measure of personal leadership than authenticity. A leader who is real, genuine, and transparent creates a high-performing environment that is open, trusting, and collaborative. In today's business world, the marketplace is littered with leaders and organizations that lack authenticity. With the instantaneous flow of information, the only way a leader stays credible is to be as authentic as possible. Take time to challenge the authenticity of your behavior: Did I really show up today, expressing what I needed to get across? Did I really live my values and purpose? Did I hold back too much? Did I risk my vulnerability enough? Also, take time to challenge your authentic self-awareness: Do I really understand my strengths and use them fully? Do I really comprehend my weaknesses? Do I have the courage to be real with myself and others about these strengths and vulnerabilities? As you pause to stretch and deepen your authenticity, your credibility and leadership voice will be strengthened.

Pause Point:
Visioning Personal Leadership Growth

Imagine yourself fully on-purpose, living your mission with optimal passion, influence, and character. See yourself fully aware and fearless about your strengths and vulnerabilities. You are standing firmly on your two feet, rooted in a deep awareness of who you are. You are determined to grow to the next level, fully aware and accepting of who you are. You know the difference you want to make in the world and possess a role that allows you to do so. You are clear about your character attributes and embody them most of the time. Pause and reflect on these questions:

o How does this vision feel?

o How close are you to this vision?

o What actions do you need to take to get there?

o What is something you can begin doing today to move towards this vision?

CHAPTER THREE

PAUSE TO
GROW OTHERS

BALANCING CARE
AND DRIVE

EARLY IN MY EXECUTIVE COACHING CAREER, I had the good fortune to advise some of Vince Lombardi's Super Bowl Champion Green Bay Packers. This legendary team is recognized by many as one of the greatest American football teams in history. Although the former players I was coaching had transitioned to business careers, Lombardi's influence was still very present in their lives and in their leadership.

I had always viewed Lombardi as the iconic, hard-driving, hard-nosed football coach. However, I did not know the person behind the coach, the person who was passionate about growing each team member in a highly intimate and personal way. On separate occasions, each of the former players surprised me with similar sentiment about Lombardi: "I have never been so loved by someone outside my family. We all knew he would do anything for us . . . *anything*. We would go through walls for this man."

Coach Lombardi earned the right to drive the talent of his players to the limit because his intense drive was balanced by his equally intense caring. He awakened in his players the respect, drive, and caring he held within himself. *When people know that a leader cares, know that a leader is in it for them, great things are possible.*

One might call this deep, connected, emotionally intelligent leadership "caring directness." We are most effective as leaders, and as developers of talent, when people first know that we genuinely care, that we are totally invested, completely committed to them. Then, and only then, do we earn the right to set very high expectations, motivate them in a sustained manner, and drive them to unleash their full potential. While it may not be politically correct or comfortable to use the word *love* in a business context, developing others is a transformative, purposeful pursuit that leverages the power of love into enduring drive and achievement.

> *Ultimately, the true test of sustainable leadership and organizational success goes beyond the amount of revenue and profit produced; the real measure of leadership is the character and quality of the people the leader and the organization produces.*

Lombardi understood that the deep emotional connection each team member felt multiplied each player's own sense of purpose and connection to something larger . . . to a higher, more team-focused purpose. Purpose-fueled connection is the glue of leadership, bonding parts and revealing wholeness. One CEO shared with me, "We all know what it is like when we love what we do, when we love the company we're connected to, when we love the products or services we represent, and when we love the people with whom we work. This powerful, energetic connection drives us to higher performance and more effective, enlightened leadership. We are usually embarrassed to acknowledge it, but love, leadership, and high performance are intimately connected. In fact, love is what deeply connects and activates them all."

However, many leaders and organizations do not pause to generate such care for their talent. Ram Charan and Bill Conaty, authors of *The Talent Masters: Why Smart Leaders Put People before Numbers*, explain it this way: "If businesses managed their money as carelessly as they manage their people, most would be bankrupt. The great majority of companies that control their finances don't have any comparable processes for developing leaders or even pinpointing which ones to develop."

Managers perceive people as a resource, a cost to be cut or an asset to be optimized; leaders see people as a source, a potential generator of energy, innovation, and purpose.

LESS IS MORE

During the writing of this book, I was working with an executive in China who was working on pause practices to accelerate his goal of developing leadership in others. He surprised me with this perceptive insight. "Kevin, leadership is like cooking a fish. One takes time to choose a high-quality fish. One treats the fish in a delicate manner, and once one begins preparing the fish, it is best not to interfere too much. It is very important not to overcontrol it or overwork it. It is best to start cooking, step back, turn it once, and let it finish. It is the Taoist principle of Wu Wei, the principle of least action. See the work. Do the work. Don't interfere too much. Success comes by doing just enough, not too much." My client made a personal connection to a deeper life principle that gave profound meaning to his own leadership growth and to mine. In growing others, particularly high-potential talent, often less is more.

A while ago, a CEO came to my office and it immediately became apparent that he was "overcooking his fish"! Pounding my desk to punctuate each passionate sentence, his fists were sending shock waves through my desk and through me. "I wish other people were as OPEN as I am." *Thump! Thump!* He was obviously passionate about openness! While he believed in openness, he did not *act openly*; he did not embody openness in his behavior. His behavior demonstrated he was *open* to being right. He was *open* to being the smartest person in the room. He was *open* to dominating discussions. He was *openly* critical. However, he was closed to his impact on others. He was closed to listening, closed emotionally, closed to collaboration. The remedy? Pause . . . stepping back to receive more and send less, to be more receptive and interfere less. Over a few months, we helped him to pause to align his verbal passion for openness with his behaviors. He paused into seeing himself and his dominant style through the eyes of others. Because he was so willing, he learned to pause to listen and hear what others were trying to contribute. He learned to pause to give others a chance to work out solutions to problems and to express their own ideas. He mastered the pause practice of asking questions to elicit awareness, collaboration, and innovation. He paused to deal with his fear and limiting beliefs. He learned the art of *slowing down the movie* to reconnect to himself, others, and the creative process. He paused to begin a rewrite of the script of his leadership behaviors and aspirations by fostering the art of authenticity, being genuine within himself and in his relationships with others. He was now authoring a new way of leading and a new way of living, and he was genuinely more open. Even his spouse noticed the change and called our office to say, "Whatever you are doing, please keep it up!" That's a notable sign. When leadership development begins to migrate to all areas of life, there's a lot more going on than an external change inspired by a tip or technique; it is real sign of transformation.

Yet, even after his spouse had called us with her enthusiastic support, he still had not fully absorbed the behavior change that was taking place. "What is going on? My team is challenging me. Suddenly, people are coming up with fresh ideas. They have never been so energized, engaged, and open. I sense something mysterious emerging in our culture. What is it?" Amused, I responded, "The 'mystery' is you. You paused into yourself and into others. As you unlocked your potential, you unleashed the organizational potential as well. You wanted openness, and you stepped back to elicit it. You became open, and now it is safe and exciting for others to follow your authentic lead. You became what you wanted to see in others; now others are rushing in to become it, too."

Pause is the most fundamental process underlying personal and organizational transformation. All leadership assessment, leadership feedback, leadership development, and leadership coaching are catalyzed by pause. In fact, if done properly, they are all pause practices. This process of stepping back for reflection moves us to greater humility, courage, and confidence, which we sustain through openness, trust, and mutual respect. This rich mixture moves us to integration, synergy, and innovation. Pause prepares a fertile field of possibility, where something new can grow inside and out.

THE POWER
OF SYNERGY

Sometimes pause feels a bit magical, like we are in the "zone," when every member of the team brings forth his or her best talents and effort, and working together we create something greater, more surprising and spectacular than we could ever do on our own. This kind of leadership requires a humility and confidence that is coupled with ambition and a sense of larger purpose that Jim Collins, researcher and author of *Good to Great*, recognized in "Level V Leaders." These leaders move ego aside, lead with character, and create a platform that invites others to perform and star. They generously open up space for everyone to shine. Dale Chihuly, the artist and designer of breakthrough glass-blowing techniques, is also known for his talent as a leader of astounding artistic collaborations. He brings together teams of distinguished glass artists to innovate astonishingly new forms, often massive pieces of glass created by working together and pushing previously held boundaries. Their productions, with Chifuly as visionary and director, and featuring many talented artists, are operatic in nature. They are the embodiment of synergy.

Karen Kimsey-House, CEO of Coaches Training Institute, the world's largest trainer of coaches, described that special connection or synergy this way: "When we are all connected to each other and our purpose, the whole transcends the parts." Karen shared a great story of how her intuition to pause energized her team and ultimately catalyzed their synergy. She and her team were seated around the table for a strategizing and curriculum-planning session. "I could feel something was off. Everyone was stressed to the max. I could tell that whatever was on their minds and in their hearts was in the way." Wisely, Karen suggested that everyone take a deep breath and step back for a little while. She asked, "What's really going on? How are you feeling? Are there some things we need to talk about? Is there something important that I am missing here?" Around the table they went, and one by one each leader talked about whatever was topmost on his or her mind. Some people were feeling overwhelmed, others were grieving recent changes, and others were feeling disconnected and anxious. Karen had the courage and insight to realize that everyone needed to reconnect to themselves, to each other, and to their common purpose. The process took about 30 minutes. Having taken that time to connect, their creativity, energy, and resources were available again. They were able to refocus wholeheartedly on their work because they connected to the value of what they create together and its potential impact on the world. Karen added, "We were able to do all that, return to our strategizing and curriculum planning, and we ended up finishing even earlier than expected. That's what taking the time to reconnect can do." As Mahatma Gandhi counseled, "There is more to life than simply increasing its speed."

> *The art of management is consistently,*
> *efficiently achieving results; the art of*
> *leadership is growing people to produce*
> *enduring value.*

As critical as technology, strategy, systems, and processes are to organizational success, our biggest leadership bets, our most important bets, are on people. Research conducted by the Corporate Executive Board has demonstrated the tangible, dramatic impact of leader-led development. Leaders, who took the time to take an active, primary role in the development of people, were 1.5 times more likely to exceed their financial goals than those who didn't. Pausing to develop people accelerates business performance. As one very experienced global CEO imparted, "Developing others appreciates our most renewable, enduring, value-creating asset—people."

CREATE A CULTURE OF CONTINUOUS INVESTMENT AND GROWTH IN PEOPLE

Leaders foster accelerated growth: growth of revenue, growth of market share, growth of profit, growth of purpose, growth of innovation, growth of contribution. The essential growth questions to pause on are

o Where does all this growth originate?

o What is the prime mover of growth?

o What fuels growth in the first place?

Too often, we view growth as merely an *external process*, rarely pausing deeply to consider its *source* within us and within our organizations. We excel at measuring growth but do we slow down, step back and consider where growth comes from?

Human insight, human energy, and human agility are the prime movers of growth in people and organizations.

> *Managers activate systems and processes for control; leaders catalyze human potential to multiply impact.*

A senior leader in a multinational consumer products company, known in the industry for her exceptional creativity, put it this way: "Creativity and innovation are mental aspirations until human heart and human engagement are activated. No amount of brilliant strategy and brilliant leadership can outperform the human spirit. Managers and technical experts must engage their mental faculties to make a difference. Effective leaders go to the primal source of achievement, growing people to grow organizations, to grow enduring results."

Like most high-achieving leaders, she did not always see herself or her role from this perspective.

Early in my career, I saw myself as the prime mover of achievement. When a job needed doing or expertise was required, I provided it. Having built my credibility through consistent achievement, as I moved up the ladder, I continued this same

'I am the one' mentality. I hit the wall in my first big role running a $1 billion region. I had hit my capacity for heroic, personally driven achievement. Honestly, I was forced to take a new path. I had no choice but to trust, let go, and become a coach and developer of people. Shifting my focus from *me* to *we* was transformative. I now estimate more than 80 percent of my role revolves around people and talent development to directly support the strategy. Helping my people to 'step back to step up' is my real job now.

Growing Others Begins with Self-Growth

Most change begins with self-change, and most growth begins with self-growth. Therefore, if you did not reflect thoroughly enough in the previous chapter, "Pause to Grow Personal Leadership," it's time to go back . . . take a deeper pause . . . and get clear there first. No amount of growing others will compensate for a leader's lack of self-growth. As enterprise leaders, our own advancing personal growth directly influences the dynamic capacity for organizational growth. Before we can grow authenticity and purpose in others, we *must* dedicate ourselves to our own growth of authenticity and purpose. If we do, our development of others will be powerful, and our credibility will be well earned. We must become the leader we wish to see in our organizations, and from this credible, solid platform, we can then accelerate the development of others.

Grounded in your personal awareness of your character, your values, your purpose, your transcendence, and your authenticity, you will have a solid frame of reference for encouraging others to join you on the growth journey. As you grow and value growth, others will follow.

Become the Leader You Wish to See in Others

A CEO of a global company deeply believed in leadership development and invested heavily in a variety of programs. He put his thumbprint on the programs, introducing the key ones as the kickoff speaker. Unfortunately, endorsing leadership development isn't enough; his daily leadership behavior ran contrary to the principles represented in the programs. Not surprisingly, the leadership programs had disappointing ROI. Additionally, retention of key players was much below expected levels. Frustrated, the CEO began to doubt the value of his investment. In one sense, he was right: the programs were not working optimally, and the investment was not paying off. However, the cause of the low ROI was not the programs; it was his own lack of participation and personal growth, his lack of embodiment of the learning. Once, to his credit, he began to take responsibility for his self-generated growth and change, word got around the organization that "leadership development is serious business for all of us." As one up-and-coming manager put it, "If the CEO works so hard on his own development, I need to do my part." ROI increased on leadership development. Become the leader and the learner you wish to see in your leadership programs, and people will join you on the development journey.

Centuries ago, Seneca wrote, "Retire into yourself as much as possible. Associate with people who are likely to improve you. Welcome those whom you are capable of improving. The process is a mutual one." Pause on this thought:

> *The best time to influence your next generation*
> *of talent is about three years before you hire*
> *them. The leadership development we engage*
> *in now, personally and organizationally, will*
> *influence both current and future generations*
> *of leaders.*

Before we move forward into how to develop others, let's step back . . . take a pause to reflect on what you already know and have experienced in this area of growth.

Pause Point:
Leadership Development Audit

Sit back . . . take a break. Think about your experiences coaching, mentoring, and growing people. Think about the highlights for yourself and others. Then, reflect on these questions:

○ What have been your most effective ways to grow people?

○ How strong are the leadership development processes and programs in your organization? Do they prepare people for the rigors of leadership and the challenges of your new strategy?

○ Who are the people you can stretch in your organization into new, first-time assignments and expect success?

○ Do you *really* know your talent inside and out? Do you see their performance and potential? Do you know their motivation and values? Do you know what energizes them and drains their energy?

Important: Be courageous and honest with your answers; your personal and organizational success hinge upon an accurate assessment.

THE LANGUAGE OF GROWING OTHERS: THE LANGUAGE OF PAUSE

The two most valuable pause tools for fostering the growth of others are *questions* and *listening*. Questions are the expressive, probing language for growing others; listening is the receptive, facilitating language for growing others. These two complementary approaches form a continuous growth conversation loop. The deeper the questions, the deeper the listening; the deeper the listening, the deeper the next question. As we dig together with each tool, we mutually excavate new discoveries. As a result, the learning is never one-sided; it is a co-created process that engenders empathy, trust, and collaboration.

The Power of Authentic Questions

Coauthors Eric Vogt, Juanita Brown, and David Isaacs wrote in *The Art of Powerful Questions*, "The usefulness of the knowledge we acquire and the effectiveness of the actions we take depend on the quality of the questions we ask. Questions open the door to dialogue and discovery. They are an invitation to creativity and breakthrough thinking." As we turn our attention to understanding more about the art and science of creativity and innovation, we learn that questions are also the keys to discovery. In *The Innovator's DNA*, coauthors Jeff Dyer, Hal Gregersen, and Clayton Christensen discern from their analysis that "innovators are consummate questioners who show a passion for inquiry. Their queries often challenge the status quo. They ask questions to understand: how things are; why they are; how they might be changed or disrupted." As a result, they discover "new insights, connections, possibilities, and directions." What's more, innovators have a high "Q/A ratio." "Their questions not only outnumber answers in a typical conversation, but are valued at least as highly as good answers." Authentic questions open up the doorway to authentic growth and development in others.

Leaders Pause to Ask Powerful Questions

Innovators working on solving problems and coming up with creative solutions rely on crafting the right questions. Leaders who are helping others to grow and innovate are always trying to craft the best questions to make a difference. Not only do innovators make asking questions an integral part of their lives, and ask more questions than non-innovators, they also ask more provocative ones . . . questions that provoke deep insight and understanding. Developing other leaders through questioning not only helps them grow, but it forces them to own their unique learning experiences.

A chairman of a global 100 firm shared with me, "At early stages of our career, we build credibility by having the answers. At later career stages, we build credibility by having the most powerful questions." Questions can "flip the VUCA forces" from volatility to vision, from unpredictability to understanding, from complexity to clarity, and from ambiguity to agility. Questions reveal to us and to others the unseen, the unknown, and the hidden. Questions unlock the door to new possibilities, new learning, and new ways to see ourselves and the world.

Questions activate the catalytic power of pause
to help us grow.

PAUSE POINT:
THE POWER OF QUESTIONS

Imagine yourself in your next team meeting. Observe and check your impulses to be the expert, the problem solver, or the holder of the most seasoned experiences and perspectives. See yourself using questions more to:

○ Challenge yourself to look at solutions from a different point of view.

○ Stay in the state of curiosity longer to sort out where others are coming from.

○ Probe deeper into motivations, perspectives, and experiences.

○ Bring the "unspeakable" question to the surface.

○ Challenge the status quo to move the conversation to the next level.

○ Build on what is being said and take it one or two steps further.

○ Engage with people at a deeper level.

What would be the impact to your team and organization if you leveraged the power of questions more? What would happen if you used your drive, analytical capabilities, and intelligence to help others to grow versus having the answers and solving the problems?

The Power of Authentic Listening

Following an extended period of international travel and organizational stress involving the shutting down of operations globally, an extremely self-confident, expressive senior executive lost her voice. She didn't just have a common cold; she had full-blown laryngitis. Unable to speak for 60+ days, she was forced to step back and listen. Her perception of her team changed radically. She saw her staff much more involved, expressive, and creative. Discussions were more uninhibited, free flowing, and creatively productive. Over time, she found that even her contributions of flip chart scribbles occasionally got in the way. "Listening showed me a way to do less but accomplish more. My team understands my vision, expectations, and values. I realize that what I need to do is discipline myself now to listen more and interfere less."

> *Questions without authentic listening*
> *are thinly veiled challenges, judgments,*
> *and assertions; challenging questions with*
> *authentic listening activates latent power,*
> *potential, and collaboration.*

How often do we pause to be genuinely present with someone? How often do we really hear what the other person is saying and feeling versus filtering it heavily through our own immediate concerns and time pressures? Authentic listening is not easy. We hear the words, but rarely do we really slow down to listen and to *squint with our ears* to hear the emotions, fears, and underlying concerns.

Effective leaders speak to influence and motivate; exceptional leaders listen to learn, collaborate, and innovate. Of all the core competencies critical to sustained leadership, listening is at, or near, the top of the list. As the thirtieth U.S. president, Calvin Coolidge, put it, "No man has ever listened himself out of a job." Despite its value-creating properties, listening is rare for many leaders, and this lack of listening is one of the key reasons leaders derail.

Research confirms that a startling 67 percent of new leaders in organizations fail within eighteen months. Why? Lack of listening. Why do teams usually break down? Poor listening. Why do relationships in general fail? Inadequate listening. According to recent research published by Kelly See, Elizabeth Wolfe Morrison, Naomi Rothman, and Jack Soll in *Organizational Behavior and Human Decision Processes*, the picture does not get any prettier. Leaders, in general, were found to be poor listeners. In fact, across four different studies, it's been shown that the greater the position of power the more elevated the propensity to discount advice, mainly due to inflated self-confidence. Too often, we as leaders are more confident in our own expertise and our past experience than trusting of others and their more current experience and insights. This lack of listening can be further complicated by a tendency of team members to defer to more senior people with perceived expertise. In "Learning When to Stop Momentum" in *MIT Sloan Management Review,* researchers Michelle Barton and Kathleen Sutcliffe explain that it is just as common for members of firefighting teams to defer to senior members because of perceived expertise. Dynamic changes and better outcomes occur when leaders stop momentum by creating interruptions to reexamine and revaluate the plan in light of current information and genuinely urge team members—through pause, questions, and listening—to speak up and voice their concerns.

We have observed three common pitfalls that inhibit people from stepping back for authentic listening:

LISTENING PITFALL 1: HYPER SELF-CONFIDENCE When we see ourselves as the quintessential expert, the most experienced or accurate person in the room, we position ourselves to fall into a listening black hole. Others with valuable insights defer rather than speak up, diminishing rather than strengthening leadership teams. The kiss of death for collaboration, connection, and innovation is moving too quickly to our own perceived "right" answer. Slow down, and challenge yourself to pause and to listen a few minutes longer to move from transaction or hyperaction to transformation.

LISTENING PITFALL 2: IMPATIENCE AND BOREDOM When conversations or meetings don't reflect our point of view or are not intellectually challenging enough, we may get impatient or bored. Our inner voice, drowning out other voices in the room, says, "They are not getting it!" They may not be getting your idea, personal framework, or solution, but they are getting something, possibly something valuable but hidden to you. If we are too caught up in our judgmental self-conversation, we can never really genuinely listen and hear what is going on around us. We lose on multiple levels: we don't learn; we don't know what is happening; we don't connect; and we don't innovate. Fight your impatience and boredom by looking deeper. Pause to question: What are they seeing and understanding that I don't see? What are the beliefs underneath what is being said?

What are the hopes and fears underneath the surface? If you stepped back and looked at things in this new or different way, what would be the implications? Stretch yourself mentally and emotionally to stay engaged by looking deeper. Remember, you can always disagree or reframe the conversation later, but as St. Francis advised, "Seek first to understand."

LISTENING PITFALL 3: BIAS FOR ACTION Sometimes listening is challenging because we want to do something, not just hear about it. Our hyperactive impulses derive from our certainty that we know the solution and reactively want to implement it. However, as a senior leader, when facing complexity and/or a maturing team, it isn't always optimal to rush in with the answers, unintentionally creating dependency, stunting the growth of others, and sacrificing transformative breakthroughs. Pause a bit longer to let groups struggle and strain more as they explore ideas, options, and deeper solutions. Listen to how they are collaborating, resolving conflict, and problem solving. Give introverts space to speak up. Step back more and step in only when absolutely necessary.

> *Managers take action quickly to advance the organization; leaders listen deeply to activate latent energy and possibility.*

Balancing Self Confidence and Humility

Recently, I was advising a CEO and his senior team in a talent review process. The CEO was extremely supportive of one up-and-coming talent. To challenge him, I asked, "Why are you so 'in love' with this candidate?" His response: "He knows precisely when to be self-confident and when to be humble." An insightful comment. Knowing when to assert our own point of view and knowing when to listen is the mark of both heightened self-awareness and great leadership. Exceptional leaders know when to be receptive—to be humble, listen, and learn—and when to be assertive. Humility keeps leaders open to learning; confidence compels leaders to serve, share, and create value. Leaders need to do both. Most of us, however, overdo self-confidence and underdo humility. As a result, our listening suffers. Without an appropriate level of humility, we will never listen. Why should we? We already have the answers!

Pausing to listen to the needs, concerns, and aspirations of our key people is crucial to growing talent. If you find yourself rushing about from meeting to meeting, project to project, and rarely pausing to check in with your key people, your team and organizational risk is mounting. Having deeper developmental discussions, really engaging people, communicates care and connection. *Pausing for developmental dialogue elevates the business conversation from management tactics to leadership excellence.*

Authentic listening is not the same as waiting for the other person to finish speaking. Peter Senge offers an interesting metaphor for how we might think of preparing to deeply listen. He refers us to a story of a gate in Jerusalem that is so narrow it is called the "eye of the needle." The only way for a camel to pass through the gate was for it to stoop and unload its baggage. Imagining ourselves at the "eye of the needle" gate and metaphorically unloading our "baggage" or opening our minds may be helpful when we want to be certain that we are actively and authentically listening.

Try practicing authentic listening. Be with people and have the goal to fully understand the thoughts and feelings they are trying to express. Use your questions and comments to draw them out, to open them up, and to clarify what is said rather than expressing your view, closing them down, and saying only what you want. Not only will this help you to understand the value and contribution the other person brings, it will create a new openness in the relationship that will allow you to express yourself and be heard more authentically as well.

Authentic listening creates the platform for true synergy and team effectiveness. Valuing and attending to different perspectives from diverse sources results in a more complete understanding of issues and more elegant solutions. *Authentic listening is the soul of growing others.*

Listening in a VUCA World

Thomas Friedman, author and *New York Times* columnist, has brilliantly elucidated that the world we live in today is being rapidly changed by the "democratization of information" at the transformational intersection of globalization and technology. As a result, regimes that take a heavy-handed, top-down approach, rarely, if ever, listening to their constituencies, are finding it increasingly difficult to survive this lightning-fast marshalling of the masses through technology. The same is true in business organizations. Before CEOs leave meetings, the tweeting, texting, and e-mailing goes global with support or resistance being nearly instantaneous. "The days of leading countries or companies via a one-way conversation are over," says Dov Seidman, CEO of LRN and author of *How: Why How We Do Anything Means Everything*. "The old system of 'command and control'—using carrots and sticks—to assert power is fast becoming replaced by 'connect and collaborate'—to generate power *through* people." Emphasizing the transforming dynamic of authentic listening, Seidman writes, "Now you have to have a two-way conversation that connects deeply to your citizens or customers or employees." As Friedman writes, "The role of the leader now is to get the best coming up from below and then meld it with a vision from above."

> *Mixing the receptive art of listening with*
> *the expressive art of visionary leadership is*
> *the alchemic formula for enduring success in*
> *today's information-rich, flat world.*

On the power and potential of listening, Peter Senge says:

> To listen fully means to pay close attention to what is being said beneath the words. You listen not only to the "music," but to the essence of the person speaking. You listen not only for what someone knows, but for what he or she is. Ears operate at the speed of sound, which is far slower than the speed of light the eyes take in. Generative listening is the art of developing

deeper silences in yourself, so you can slow your mind's hearing to your ears' natural speed, and hear beneath the words to their meaning.

MERGING THREE INTERRELATED PAUSES FOR GROWING OTHERS

For growth to have a lasting, transformative impact, three interrelated pauses that arise from questioning and listening need to merge: *building awareness, building commitment,* and *building practice.* If all three are present and informing one another, breakthroughs will occur and growth will be sustained. If we do not help others to sufficiently pause for each of these phases, the results will most likely dissipate over time.

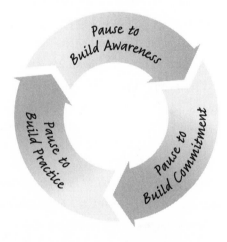

Three Interrelated Growth Pauses

Growing Others Pause 1: Use Questions and Listening to Build Awareness

As we experienced through the previous chapter of this book, "Pause to Grow Personal Leadership," leadership growth begins with self-awareness—knowing yourself, what is important to you, aligning with your purpose, and understanding how your actions or inactions, strengths or weaknesses affect others. As leaders, we are continually faced with the task of also building outside-in awareness. Awareness of changing market conditions, emerging economic realities, new capital needs, cost concerns, and operational issues dominate our time and attention. But often the greatest task of Pausing for Awareness is in the human, interpersonal domain. People problems are typically quite complex, yet when people in conflict come to us with their concerns, we often slip into a reactive, knee-jerk mode and look for a fast, transactive fix.

To help people grow, stay out of the expert, mentor role, and pause to help people sort out their current situations. Build awareness by using questions and listening to help others sort out a variety of internal or external challenges. Questions you might use to assist people in building awareness include:

- Would you tell me more about yourself (this person, the problem, or situation)? What is the background? What are the challenges? What are the key issues?
- What is the current state of the situation? If you faced this head-on and objectively, what is the current situation you face?
- What are some connections from the past to this current situation, pattern, belief, attitude, or behavior?
- What have you learned about yourself and your reactions?
- What beliefs, values, or insights came up for you?
- How are your strengths and growth area playing out in this situation?
- Had you taken another approach, how could you see yourself (this person, the problem, or situation) in a new light?
- What clarity have you gained?
- What new clarity needs to surface?

Growing Others Pause 2: Use Questions and Listening to Build Commitment

Awareness opens up the possibility for a higher level of performance. However, awareness and insight by themselves are not enough. If they were, we would not have the same New Year's resolutions each year! Moving toward enduring leadership effectiveness requires motivation born of emotional commitment. Building commitment begins with helping people to consider the consequences of their actions. However, it is not enough to help others to understand *intellectually* that if they continue on the same course, they're going to fall short of their goals, limit themselves or others. We have to help people to *feel and experience it*. When we have a deep emotional connection to the impact of a behavior or decision, our life can change permanently. This is why trauma can be such a great change-producing teacher. Noel Tichy and Warren Bennis put it this way: "Courageous leaders often get their courage from their fear about what will happen if they don't step up and boldly step out."

In the 2011 film *The Descendents*, George Clooney plays Matt King, a husband and father who puts work first. Although he shares a home with his wife and daughters, he has been absent from their lives. In an early scene in the movie, Matt sits in his wife's hospital room. She has been in a boating accident that has left her in a coma for three weeks. Finally absorbing the reality of the situation and hoping he can transform it by being a better husband and father, Matt blurts out, "I'm ready to change. I'm ready to be a real husband and a real father." As "the back-up parent," Matt doesn't know his daughters or what to do with them. The realities of the unfolding tragedy bring all this into focus because he is finally feeling and seeing what is going on around him. As the plot progresses, he understands the consequences of his entrenched behavior, and commitment dawns. He starts listening to his daughters, to others, and to his inner voice. Clooney's character comes to a sharp realization of what is most important to him. Once we clearly perceive and emotionally experience both the upside and downside consequences of a behavior, meaningful commitment to transformation—boldly stepping out—can begin. *Commitment blooms when the fear of destroying the bud is less than the incredible potentiality of the rose.*

By guiding people to grasp the life-enriching and life-damaging consequences of their current behaviors or paths, you help them to feel the creative tension between where they want to end up and where they are headed as a result of their actions. Helping people to pause and envision these alternative futures and to make new life choices is the essence of building commitment. Remember, to develop deeper commitment the person has to *see*, *feel*, and *experience* these consequences for himself or herself, not just adopt your version of the consequences.

Build commitment using questions and listening to facilitate a clearer understanding of the upside and downside consequences. Questions you might ask include:

- o What are the most compelling, positive reasons for you to do X?
- o What are the downsides for not doing X?
- o Can you feel the positive pull of X and the desire to avoid the downside? Do you clearly feel the tension?
- o Why is it so important to you to do this? What is the disaster scenario if you don't?
- o Will you begin doing X? By when? How often?
- o How invested are you in doing this?
- o What will you and others lose if you don't? What will you and others gain if you do?

Growing Others Pause 3: Use Questions and Listening to Build Practice

Without practice, there is no transformation. Pausing to help others identify what to practice breathes life, vitality, and momentum into their new awareness and commitment. The people we are helping to grow can be fully aware and committed to noble goals, but if we fail to consistently give them the opportunity to practice new behaviors, it is like lighting a lamp and closing our eyes.

Admiring great insights and feeling proud of new commitments will not, in themselves, propel others toward their desired destination. Lao-Tzu, who wrote the profound life and leadership text, *Tao Te Ching*, reflected, "A Sage will practice the Tao. A fool will only admire it."

> *Identifying a practice makes the possible possible; beginning a practice makes the possible probable; engaging in enduring practice makes the possible real.*

An interesting connection to *deep practice* can be found in neuroscience's understanding of myelin, an insulating material that wraps itself around neurons—a circuit of nerve fibers. Although we need synapses, it is myelin that is responsible for why we learn things and get good at them. Myelin increases the signal strength, speed, fluency, and accuracy of the synapses. The more frequently we practice, the more myelin optimizes our ability to access that new behavior or skill. Whether it is listening more deeply and asking more questions, changing your golf swing, or improving presentation skills, "Practice makes myelin makes perfect." Daniel Coyle, author of *The Talent Code*, explains it this way: "Deep practice is built on a paradox: struggling in certain targeted ways—operating at the edges of your ability, where you make mistakes—makes you smarter. . . . Experiences where you are forced to slow down, make errors, and correct them—as you would if you were walking up an ice-covered hill, slipping and stumbling as you go—end up making you swift and graceful without your realizing it."

When Pablo Casals, whom many consider the greatest cellist ever, was ninety-two years old, he was still pausing to practice his cello five hours a day—more than his students. One day a frustrated student approached Casals and asked, "Pablo, why are you practicing five hours a day? You are putting your students to shame. Why are you practicing so hard?" Evidently, Pablo responded humbly, "I'm practicing so much because I am *finally* starting to make progress!"

Consider asking the people you are leading the following questions as tools for co-creating practices to support the growth of others:

- What could you begin practicing tomorrow? What is a seemingly small behavior that could be most impactful? What could you do that would have the most beneficial impact for you and for others?
- What is something you practiced in the past that could be helpful here?
- What could you do more of, less of, or differently to impact this the most?

- Can you see yourself consistently practicing this? Daily? How often?
- When will you begin this? How often will you practice?

Pause Point:
Accelerating the Growth of Others

Step back for a moment to get prepared for deeper, more effective coaching and development conversations. Consider doing this as a stand-alone meeting or at the end of a regular business interaction. Think about using questions more, listening more, and speaking less. Try pausing to build awareness, to build commitment, and to build practices to help move the person forward. As you pause on these considerations, also ask yourself:

- How would these new behaviors alter and enhance your conversations?

- What might you discover about the other person? About yourself?

- What degree of care and commitment would you demonstrate or embody?

- What might get in your way? Expertise? Problem solving? Impatience? Fear? Or, are you moving the person too quickly into fix-it mode?

- Will you coach people more? Will you use questions and listening to build awareness, commitment and practice? When? With whom will you start? How often?

Deep Pause to Grow Leaders:
A Case Study

Since 2002, we have been fortunate to work with 800+ senior leaders at Novartis, the $58 billion life sciences company, named the number one most admired pharmaceutical company a few times over the past several years. Like many companies, Novartis faced the dilemma of how to grow and develop a stream of talented people who would emerge prepared and qualified for leadership. We distilled this challenge to two questions: (1) How can Novartis leaders step back to get to know their talent on a more intimate basis to accelerate succession decision quality? (2) How could Novartis accelerate the development of key high-potential leaders?

We addressed these questions by customizing a program that simultaneously accelerated the pace and quality of both leadership development and succession decision making. As one very perceptive Novartis sponsor put it, "I need to more intimately know our talent one to three levels below me. In talent reviews previously, I would make succession decisions based on very limited interaction. Now, I know these people very well, and I know what kind of assignments different people are ready for. I can immediately make informed, accurate career and stretch assignments." The program combined expertise in talent assessment and executive coaching with three areas critical to the development of leaders: building personal awareness and purpose; enhancing trust-based influence and teaming; and impacting real-world business challenges.

When Novartis initiated the program in 2002, the issue of developing talent within their company was critical. In 2000, they had recruited 79 percent of their talent from outside the organization. By 2002, they had improved that percentage to 58 percent, but they needed to do better. Novartis was determined "to reduce its outside hiring costs, leverage its investment in recruitment, and develop future leaders from among its existing talent pool." By 2005, and continuing to the present, only 30 percent of senior talent has been hired outside the organization. Millions of dollars were saved in recruiting. Millions more were leveraged to produce and sustain results. Novartis's commitment to its key talent has accomplished even more: it has helped create a base of self-aware, influential leaders whose focus extends beyond individual results to a concern for the team and the broader enterprise. "This is not skills training; it's about who you are and the impact that has," said Mechtild Walser-Ertel, who has participated as a talent management and organizational development leader for Novartis Consumer Health.

Leadership development programs that create lasting value connect the individual's personal beliefs, talents, and purpose with the needs of the organization and marketplace. When leaders pause to make this important connection, they emerge effective and inspired. They possess a crystalized knowledge of what they believe and what they care about, as well as how to leverage their talent specifically to impact the enterprise. The most effective leaders can articulate and embody their purpose and values. They can influence and connect effectively with others, and they can produce enduring business value. This principle of Inside-Out and Outside-In leadership development in action was completely integrated into the process and curriculum to develop Novartis leaders.

"This work is so effective at creating self-awareness," commented sponsor Juergen Brokatsky-Geiger, Novartis global head, human resources. "We wanted to bring our talent into a reflective process that allows them to think more deeply about their career aspirations and abilities and what opportunities provide the best fit. This benefits the organization as much as the specific individual." The results of this approach for coaching and development have cascaded deeply into the company:

- Participants bring their learning back into their businesses, and concepts, language, and behaviors become embodied throughout the organization.
- Depth of talent is identified and succession becomes more intimate and real, enabling better decisions on whom to develop and promote.
- Leaders grow in confidence and authenticity as they connect more deeply to who they are and what is important to the enterprise.
- Participants engage more successfully with teams and create peer-coaching and networking connections beyond the program.
- Leaders learn to collaborate on real-world leadership challenges.
- Attention broadens to create a culture that better balances business results and people development.
- Program sponsors benefit in their leadership development as much as the participants.

PAUSE POINT:
DEVELOPING OTHERS

Sit back and take a break. Think about your interactions over the past two years in developing others. Be open to your strengths, growth areas, and legacy in these areas. Consider these questions as you reflect on your experiences:

⊙ What could you do more of, less of, or differently to develop your people?

⊙ What could your organization do more of, less of, or differently?

⊙ What will your people development legacy be?

PAUSE FOR GENERATIVITY:
PAYING IT FORWARD

The great psychologist Erik Erikson studied the entire life cycle of human development and postulated that we move through eight stages in our lifetime, beginning with *trust* as an infant and advancing during our developing years to *autonomy, initiative, industry, identity,* then to *intimacy, generativity,* and *integrity* in our adult years. His observation was that in the stage he called "generativity" we do our *payback.* We pursue a desire for our life to count and have meaning, to leave a legacy to help the next generation. It is a stage of life that is no longer about us; it is about how we can serve, benefit, and grow others. Generativity is the stage when we slow down to accelerate others; we step back to pull others forward. It is our most authentic time to *lead forward* for ourselves and for other people. A generative leader gets energy and meaning by seeing others succeed. In short, we lead on-purpose, in-character and in-service, helping the next generation to go beyond us. We give what we can and experience the joy of transferring knowledge and the joy of others exceeding us.

Marc Belton, executive vice president, Global Strategy, Growth and Marketing, General Mills, thinks of generativity as legacy or "living on." He shared his holistic view of how he and his creative partner at General Mills, Mark Addicks, senior vice president, chief marketing officer, will "live on" at their company:

> You can live on by what you create and affect. You can live on through your DNA, but you also live on in people and in things that bring fundamental change. We'll live on here [General Mills]. We'll live on here because we care about doing business right, which means meeting the needs of our consumers and customers. We have a legacy of people who have been infected with things that matter—a sense of inspiration, a sense of motivation, a sense of being creative, a sense of knowing that you can bring about change when you are deeply interested in seeing something change. We will have infected a lot of people because we care, and we want to develop people, because we know that's the essence. We want to develop people, and we want to bring about change. That's the culture of generative innovation.

The key development breakthrough of growing oneself is self-awareness and authenticity; the key development breakthrough of growing others is service and generativity. Winston Churchill once said, "We make a living by what we get; we make a life by what we give." Be a generative leader. . . . Pause to accelerate the growth of others.

Step Back to Lead Forward: Seven Pause Practices to Grow Others

Pause to Grow Others Practice 1: Be On-Purpose

Helping key people to get clear on their most meaningful, compelling aspiration may be our greatest developmental gift as a leader. We can talk about an achievement-driven legacy all day long, but a purpose-driven legacy, one that inspires clarity of contribution, is the real achievement. Take time with people to assist in clarifying core talents and core values. Then, ask, "With these talents and these values, what is the difference you want to make?" Help people to crystalize their purpose to a few, potent words so its profound simplicity can be an ever-present guide. Once they clarify their purpose, help people to apply it as a development tool. Ask, "Were you aligned with your purpose in that meeting? How could you have demonstrated your values or used your talents more effectively?" Helping to get clear on purpose and applying it as a practical development guide is a direct route to authentic leadership development.

Pause to Grow Others Practice 2: Question and Listen

Use questions and listening to build awareness, build commitment, and build practice. Hold back your expertise and stay present with questions and listening to keep the pressure and accountability squarely on the person you are advising. Your job is to question and listen to foster clarity within the person, not to resolve their challenges from your perspective. Pause within yourself to access the most powerful questions, and use pause to deeply listen rather than filling the space with your voice. Pause inside for the best questions, pause outside to listen deeply, and the growth conversation will be the most profound.

Pause to Grow Others Practice 3: Risk Experimentation

Growing others is a co-created process of hypothesizing, experimenting, and exploring options together. Step back with key people to explore possible stretch assignments collaboratively: "Have you considered this possibility? What about that possibility? What would you need to develop and to prepare to take that on? Are you ready now?" With highly learning agile people, take the risk to experiment with big stretches; you may be surprised how well they do. Similarly, step back to co-create, building practices together. "If you want to develop better platform skills, what are some ways you would be motivated to do this? Since broader enterprise leadership is crucial for you, what current enterprise initiatives would you want to take on?" Risk experimentation with key people by co-creating the practices and/or stretch assignments together.

Pause to Grow Others Practice 4: Reflect and Synthesize

Take time to reflect on the experience, expertise, strengths, vulnerabilities, talents, motivations, and values of your people. Reflect on each person deeply so that you can see each individual as a whole person . . . as a whole leader. What do you see? What is her performance? What is her potential? Am I limiting him because of my limited perception or my own performance anxiety? What do others see in him that I am missing?

Consider engaging in a deep talent discussion to map people according to a performance-potential grid, getting assessment and feedback to ground your own perceptions. The deeper you pause to reflect and understand your talent, the greater the possibilities for them and for your organization. Invest more time reflecting on the strengths and development needs of your key people.

Pause to Grow Others Practice 5: Consider Inside-Out and Outside-In Dynamics

Take an honest look at how your organization develops talent. Are your leadership development programs too Outside-In, mainly leveraging 360° assessments and business topics? Are your programs fully leveraging Inside-Out self-awareness with strategically relevant Outside-In business content? Take the time to ensure that your time invested in developing people has a good balance of personal insight from the Inside-Out and business-relevant content from the Outside-In.

Grow Others Pause Practice 6: Foster Generativity

Stepping back to coach, develop, and transfer knowledge is the very essence of generativity. Coaching and mentoring are important processes, but generativity, equipping the next generation to flourish, is the critical outcome. Shift more of your time to this fulfilling and energizing pursuit. Imagine yourself at earlier stages of your career, getting the help and advice you needed. Aren't these the people and leaders you most remember? Those generous leaders paused from their hectic schedules and patiently helped us sort out our challenges.

The true measure of your leadership will not turn out to be your great achievements, but the number of great leaders you turn out.

Pause to Grow Others Practice 7: Be Authentic

Growing others requires deep authenticity: authentic questions, authentic listening, authentic presence, authentic knowledge transfer, and authentic generativity. The more you become what you are encouraging others to be, the greater your credibility, voice, and influence. Be clear about what you know and what you don't know. Be honest with what you can help develop and what you cannot. Be open and authentic with your people, and they will be open and authentic with you. Share your authentic stories—the triumphs, the challenges, and the failures—and your people will step forward with their most genuine, value-creating selves as well. Be a co-learner with your team, and they will join the learning journey with you.

> *Be the change you wish to see in your*
> *organization.*

Pause Point:
Visioning the Growth of Others

Imagine your organization rising up with incredible performance and realized potential. You have several successors ready to advance the organization to the next level. These people see you as the most valued coach-mentor-advisor in their careers. Many say, "I could not have gotten here without him/her. I am in this position largely because of his/her investment in my growth as a leader." You can see this next generation take over and lead the organization to new possibilities. They are ready, full of energy and shared purpose. Take a moment and consider these questions:

○ How does this vision make you feel?

○ How close are you to this vision as a reality?

○ What do you need to do to get there?

○ What actions can you begin taking today?

CHAPTER FOUR

PAUSE TO GROW CULTURES OF INNOVATION

THE WORLD BELONGS TO THE INNOVATIVE

GREAT THINKERS, SCIENTISTS, ARTISTS, AND LEADERS move the world forward by stepping back; the higher the quality of pause, the greater the creative possibility. Albert Einstein, like other exceptional innovators, practiced deep reflection to probe the latent patterns of life. His assistant, Banesh Hoffman, described his profound way of penetrating reality:

His powers of focus had a great intensity and depth. When struggling with a recalcitrant problem, he was haunted as if hunting animal prey. Often, when he faced a seemingly insolvable difficulty, he crossed the room with long strides, while a finger was wrapped in a strand of long gray hair. A look, dreaming and distant had a distinct inward presence. There was no appearance of concentration, no frowning, only a quiet, intimate communion. Einstein suddenly stopped. He had found the solution! Sometimes the solution was so simple we felt like slapping our faces! The magic had worked invisible in its depth.

Einstein blended his incredible intelligence and expertise with deep pause to comprehend an entirely new way to see the deeper realities of our existence. Walter Isaacson, author of the biography, *Einstein: His Life and Universe*, would have us remember that "what made Einstein special was his impertinence, his nonconformity, and his distaste for dogma." He tells us that it was his great intellect, body of knowledge, tenacious focus, as well as his curiosity, observance, rebelliousness, skepticism, and his willingness to wrestle with a paradox for a long time, that led him from a "thought experiment" at age sixteen to two unconnected postulates, and eventually, to the theory of relativity. Although it came to him in a classic *Eureka!* moment, it was the culmination of ten years of persistent study combined with reflection. Isaacson, who was Steve Jobs's chosen biographer, has noted that Jobs and Einstein shared some common characteristics. They were both intense, creative thinkers, nonconformists, who refused to be "confined by accepted dogmas of the day." Because they were willing to discard dogmatic ideas, they were able to think differently. Einstein said, "Imagination is more important than knowledge." Neither Einstein nor Jobs could have imagined their innovations without their body of knowledge and experiences, but their daring and what Isaacson called Einstein's "impertinence" gave them the boldness to keep driving toward new possibilities.

Boldness has been the hallmark of Daniel Vasella, M.D., chairman of Novartis. He is known in the industry as the life science leader who always did the unexpected and succeeded. Asked about this reputation, he said, "Each key strategic move made over the years has come out of a reflection, an independence of thinking that was bigger than conformity. Personally and professionally, conformity is not important. What is crucial is clearly seeing situations and taking a new way. It is also crucial once one sees a new innovative way to test it out, to get both challenge and support from competent people." A few years ago, Dr. Vasella made a huge multibillion-dollar bet on a very bold, innovative move to establish an entirely new global research center, Novartis Institute of Biomedical Research (NIBR), in Cambridge, Massachusetts. With a few thousand people and drawing on the research and academic talent from MIT, Harvard, and other institutions in the area, as well as around the world, it has become the industry standard for developing great people and new compounds. Taking an entirely new approach, these researchers are following molecular pathways to reveal new, very specialized pharmaceuticals and revolutionizing the industry. Reflecting on this, Vasella shared, "What looked like a radical, revolutionary move in the industry was something that just made sense to me and to Mark Fishman, M.D., who came from academic research at Harvard to run NIBR. It was a certainty that we needed to take a new way, especially from a talent standpoint. Others saw it as innovative. To us, it just made scientific and business sense." Commenting on the challenging process of moving research staff from Switzerland to the United States, he said, "We also needed to get research free of headquarters. Innovative researchers need freedom of thought, freedom from dogma, freedom from the bureaucracy of headquarters, and space to discover. Providing the freedom to collaborate scientifically has been crucial to our innovation success."

The world belongs to the most innovative. In today's VUCA world, efficiency is the mark of management, whereas innovation is the hallmark of leadership. In fact, in today's nonstop, globally connected business climate, sustainability rests on innovation. Without incessant innovation, the wave of someone else's innovation will overtake us. Innovation is no longer merely a distinguishing difference for organizations; it is *the* enduring difference. Innovation involves embracing uncertainty and ambiguity and being willing to risk failure for the sake of learning. But where is this innovation going to come from? From the rare genius-like inventors? Or from a culture of curious learners who are so passionate, engaged, and purposeful that they can continually redefine and reinvent?

Reflecting on invention and innovation, a senior scientist in the cardiovascular division at Medtronic shared:

> Innovation is the realization of something new, possibly an invention that is considered successful, groundbreaking in its impact, and overcomes the status quo or old way of doing things. Whether you're talking about a product, service, or a theory, to become an innovation, an invention needs to be realized and change a paradigm. Darwin's theory of evolution and Einstein's theory of relativity shifted our thinking. Steve Jobs didn't invent the mp3 player or the iPod, and didn't invent the technology behind iTunes. However, he was the innovator

who made these inventions a success through great design, ease of use, and a business model that everyone could get behind. Inventions can "die on the vine," but innovations are "the fruit that makes great wine." An innovation can of course create an unfortunate outcome, such as foods that contribute to poor nutrition. Astronauts consume freeze-dried ice cream—a successful invention—during space flight. Freeze-dried ice cream is available for purchase at science museums, but this product is not an innovation. The process of freeze drying food would be an innovation, as it created a means of preserving food that was adopted by the food industry in various markets. Relative to innovation, invention is easy. Innovation is harder.

In *Theory U: Leading from the Future as It Emerges*, Otto Scharmer tells us, "All leaders and innovators, whether in business, communities, government, or non-profit organizations do what artists do: they create something new and bring it into the world. The open question is: Where do their actions come from? . . . We can't see the inner place, the *source* from which people act when . . . they operate at their highest possible level or, alternatively when they act without engagement or commitment." Scharmer identifies three levels of deeper awareness—Open Mind, Open Heart, Open Will—and says, "We cannot meet the challenges at hand if we do not change our interior condition and illuminate our blind spot—the source of our attention and action." He provokes us to understand that self-awareness is at the core of innovation. "The turbulent challenges of our time force all institutions and communities to renew and reinvent themselves. To do that, we must ask: Who are we? What are we here for? What do we want to create together?"

People think innovations are driven by high-profile individuals—the Steve Jobses, Albert Einsteins, or Thomas Edisons of the world—who create the breakthroughs for the masses. Too often, we create myths about these uniquely inventive leaders, turning them into icons. In many organizations that we study and advise, the real value-creating sources of innovation are internalized in the networks of engaged, collaborative, diverse groups of people committed to a common purpose that serves and contributes continually in new ways. As one CEO shared with me, "Even when you think someone is the genius-hero innovator, it usually turns out to have been an extremely collaborative process with many people involved and contributing and supporting the eventual breakthrough. Heroes are usually made by many competent collaborators arduously working behind the scenes." The real innovators are the *innovators of culture* who make constant creation the life force of the organization. *Inventors create product and service breakthroughs; authentic leaders foster enduring cultures of breakthrough innovation.*

Innovation is the high-performance mantra of most business gurus today. We praise the merits of innovation to our clients. We worship its virtues. We grant sainthood to the icons of innovation. The religious fervor around innovation is for good reason. In today's world, innovation is the new leadership. But as much as we laud the value-creating potential of innovation, we rarely ask ourselves, "Where does innovation come from? Where does it begin? What does it look like? How does it become embodied in the people and the culture of organizations?"

PURPOSE DRIVES INNOVATIVE CULTURES

Ray Anderson has become a legend and an inspiration. Yet, if you had heard him speak at TED in 2009, he would have told you that he is an industrial engineer, an entrepreneur, "who went from being a plunderer, a recovering plunderer, thanks to the people at Interface, to America's Greenest CEO in five years." To me, Anderson is a very authentic, very innovative leader. In 1994, at age sixty, Ray Anderson, who was then CEO and founder of Interface, Inc., changed the course of his publicly held, industry-leading, highly profitable floor-covering company. As Ray described it, "I wanted Interface, a company so oil-intensive you could think of it as an extension of the petrochemical industry, to be the first enterprise in history to become truly sustainable—to shut down the smokestacks, close off its effluent pipes, to do no harm to the environment and take nothing not easily renewed by the earth." A self-described "radical industrialist," Ray paused to reinvent his company around a clear mission of sustainability. He was determined that Interface would do well by doing good. Ray's personal leadership story is Interface's story. It is a demonstration of how an authentic leader with vision and mission can grow a culture of talented, innovative people around a common commitment to a meaningful, purposeful goal. Ray was an innovator from the get-go. He started his company in 1973 with an idea that challenged the status quo in the carpet industry. Just as Steve Jobs dared to insist that a computer could be made that was quiet and had fonts that could be beautiful, totally transforming our desktop computer experience, Ray Anderson dared to think that carpet could be made in modular squares, not only rolls, totally transforming the flooring industry.

Pausing to read a book can ignite the spark that catalyzes radical innovation. In 1994, Ray Anderson was reading Paul Hawken's book, *The Ecology of Commerce*, in preparation for a talk to an Interface task force on the company's environmental vision. They had none, and customers were questioning the company about what it was doing about the environment. When Ray read Hawken's assertion that industry leaders are not only responsible but the only ones who have the power to reverse the destruction of the biosphere, Ray experienced what he described as a "spear in the chest" epiphany, a meaningful realization of his responsibility to step forward, and a realization that one company could play a significant role in creating a model for sustainable business that others might follow. He said to himself, "Unless somebody leads no one will." That year he vowed to shift the company's strategy by changing its industrial practices and focusing on sustainability without sacrificing its business goals. His purpose was clear. He was going to do business, make money, and take responsibility for protecting the environment. Ray's vision and mission was to eliminate any negative impact Interface has on the environment by 2020. He reinvented the company, and his vision changed "every aspect of the business, creating a culture of associates who are highly adaptable to the pace of change it brought and highly committed to its success." The shared vision "flattened the organization" because a hierarchical structure would stand in the way of the purpose-driven collaboration and cooperation required.

To foster creative solutions, Interface also needed to grow a culture that encouraged openness and allowed for failure. Associates at all levels felt engaged and connected to something bigger than making carpet. Their accomplishment toward their mission has changed not only Interface but, by example, the industry. By 2011, before his death, Anderson estimated that they were more than halfway to their goal. Anderson explained that they approached the goal the way climbers reach the peak of a mountain: one step at a time. "That's how we become sustainable. Along the way we just might create an example that other companies will want to follow. We become restorative, not just by what we do but what we influence others to do as well. . . . We really began to think in different ways about our business." Good will in the marketplace soared. In addition to eliminating waste and reducing costs, the quality of their products was better than they had ever been. Ray paused to learn, to align his values, and to connect the values of his entire organization around a shared, galvanizing purpose. All of this began with a pause to answer burning customer questions and with a humble, confident, innovative leader's sense of purpose and responsibility.

Anderson lived The Pause Principle. He was willing to engage the Inside-Out/Outside-In growth dynamics as he innovated self, others, and his organizational culture. He had the courage to stop momentum and see a new way forward. He had the depth to see a greater mission to which everyone could connect their personal purpose. He had the vision to see the future emerge beyond himself. Anderson was an authentic innovator, engaging in the full scope of innovative leadership. He faced reality and then he changed it, the two required actions of authentic, purposeful, innovative leaders.

Jane Stevenson, vice chairman of Korn/Ferry's CEO & Board Services group, and coauthor with Bilal Kaafarani of *Breaking Away: How Great Leaders Create Innovation That Drives Sustainable Growth—and Why Others Fail*, shared:

> It starts at the top, but innovation is a team sport. Each person
> needs to feel that they matter, that the outcome wouldn't be the
> same without their contribution. One of the key jobs of leaders
> is to make sure each person has a clear sense of purpose and

value in connection to the larger mission. There has to be the Power of One, but there also has to be the Power of the Team, an abundance mentality, in which everyone takes the strengths of those beside them and builds on them. In this kind of collaborative, abundance mentality, there is a limitless mentality about what can be achieved.

In their book, Stevenson and Kaafarani identify four types of innovation: transformational, category, marketplace, and operational. Stevenson explained to us that all four types have value and "the portfolio helps everyone in organizations thrive." Stevenson also noted that another characteristic of innovative cultures is the genuine feeling on the part of every employee that it is a privilege to work for the customer.

As Anderson demonstrated, the key to innovation is pausing and paying attention to the endogenic forces within our organizations and ourselves that are pointing new possible ways forward. He also embodied the critical awareness of the exogenic forces happening in the arenas of competitors, customers, community, and the environment—all of which are sources of inspiration for us to serve and co-create with in new ways. How well are you listening inside-out and outside-in for the cues and clues to strategic innovation?

Pause Point:
Inside-Out and Outside-In
Forces Shaping Innovation

○ How well are you pausing to listen to the deep, fundamental change that needs to take place in your team or organization? Are you taking enough time to sort this out? Are you paying attention to what needs to happen, tough choices and all?

○ How well are you using questions and listening to draw forth the new, innovative ideas in team settings? Are you asking the extra "What if?" or "What's possible?" questions to stretch the conversation further or more deeply?

○ Are you fostering a culture of experimentation, valuing the pursuit of new, innovative breakthroughs, even when they do not succeed at times? Are you courageous enough to let failure foster learning and development?

○ How attuned are you to your emerging, future customer needs? Are you questioning and listening in a manner that goes beyond immediate needs and wants to partner with them to ensure a mutually evolving future?

○ How aware are you of your competitors' latest breakthroughs? How can your core organizational competencies take these new ideas to another level?

○ How often and how deeply do you brainstorm or question-storm with your team the game-changing scenarios inside and outside your organization?

CREATING A CULTURE OF INNOVATION

Mike Paxton, former CEO of Häagen-Dazs and recent CEO of the rapidly expanding jewelry company Chamilia, is a great example of a collaborative leader who creates cultures of innovation. Mike excels at engaging his people in the process of figuring out new, better ways to do things. He has a deep legacy of collaborative innovation from his game-changing marketing of the Pillsbury Doughboy to bringing Häagen-Dazs global, and to taking a jewelry design firm around the world. In thinking about what innovation could mean for Chamilia, Mike paused to think about how he could convey to the organization how to make continuous innovation a companywide goal. "This is a fast-growing, successful company with highly energized teams with tremendous creative design success. I had to step back to think about how I could inspire them to push the envelope, set innovation as the goal not just in design, but in all areas." Mike challenged everyone with this possibility: "Every year, starting this year, we're going to be *the* innovator in the industry." Everyone rallied around the goal. Mike had everyone, not just the design people, but the people in display, manufacturing, and the whole supply chain, challenging themselves to think differently about how they produced things in new ways. "The whole idea of innovation has transcended itself. It's now a part of the culture, and it is permeating all areas. People feel challenged in a positive way to keep growing; it's not just routine." Mike paused to create a culture of innovation.

Managers accelerate to keep pace with the competition; leaders paradoxically step back to go beyond the competition.

FAIL YOUR WAY TO INNOVATION

While rallying people around a common, compelling mission of innovation is crucial, it is also extremely critical to create an atmosphere in which experimentation and failure are seen as an ally not a threat. Most organizations aspire for innovation, but because they also do everything possible to avoid failure, they unknowingly squeeze the innovative life force out of the culture. While most organizations want innovation, they don't realize that much of what they do kills it. Seymour Cray, the godfather of the supercomputer industry, was known for his astounding ability to fail, learn, and recover. Many years ago, John Rollwagen, the former CEO of Cray Research, shared with me, "I have never seen anyone fail, recover and learn so quickly. Seymour Cray was fearless in his experimentations and lightning fast in his ability to learn from failed attempts. He visibly innovated through rapid failure."

As innovative leaders, we must have the confidence and self-trust to repeatedly risk failure, the courage and openness to absorb hard-earned learning, and the endurance to eventually break through.

When Ken Melrose was chairman and CEO of Toro, a team made a considerable investment in coming up with a new metal hood for a riding lawn mower. They hoped to save the company time and money with this new concept. Unfortunately, the project failed. Ken called the team to his office. As they gathered outside, they feared the worst, but when Ken opened the door and ushered them inside they were totally shocked to find balloons and refreshments. Ken had invited them to celebrate. "Most innovative ideas don't work out. We need to keep trusting, creating, risking, and celebrating the 'good tries'—particularly when things don't work out." Rooted in their CEO's authentic embodiment of the value of learning gained from experimentation even at the risk of failing, this "go for it" attitude pervaded the company, infusing everyone with energy, confidence, and a renewed sense of permission to innovate. *Managers do everything possible to avoid the arrival of failure; leaders accelerate through failure fueled by new learning.*

> *The fire of innovation is lit with purpose*
> *and self-innovation, spreads by igniting the*
> *spark of innovation in others, and burns*
> *continuously in a culture of innovation.*

Chapters 2 and 3 of *The Pause Principle* discuss the first two stages of innovation: Pause to Grow Personal Leadership and Pause to Grow Others. These set the stage for an authentic, open, collaborative leadership culture. These are the fundamentals for creating the new and the different. Seen from this perspective, innovation originates as an inside-out growth dynamic that has at its core self-innovation, then extends to support the innovation of others, cultures, industries, and the global community.

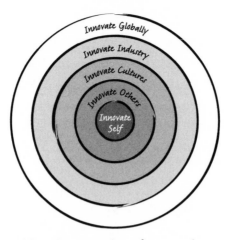

The Five Domains of Innovation

Deep from within, leaders like Ray Anderson take the leadership journey of changing themselves and then changing their cultures, industries, and the world. Wise leaders innovate self to be a worthy steward for systemic innovation. In this context, innovation is not merely coming up with the next inventive idea; it originates in the purpose-filled mission to "make a dent in the universe," as Steve Jobs said. Take a moment to reflect on your values, purpose, and mission to inform your innovation sources.

PAUSE POINT:
PURPOSE-FUELED INNOVATION

○ What bothers you most about your industry? Team? Organization? World? What could you do to "change the game"?

○ What are you most passionate about? Have you linked this passion to your purpose, strategy, behavior, and vision for innovation?

○ If you brought forth your deepest values into your leadership behaviors and strategy, what could you create or co-create with your teams?

○ At the end of your life, what do you hope others are thanking you for changing?

Partnerships, Dreaming, and Big Questions Push Innovation

Marc Belton and Mark Addicks have had long, successful, highly innovative careers at General Mills. They consider their two decades of creative partnership at "the Mills" a major element of their continuous growth and contribution. "You just can't do it yourself. You have to have creative partners and teams. Nothing gets done by the Lone Ranger." Belton and Addicks emphatically assert that you have to have partnerships both inside and outside of the company. Partnership pushes innovation. Their "First Wednesdays Forums" are designed to stimulate new thinking by listening to leaders in diverse industries. On the first Wednesday of each month, they invite leaders who are driving brands in the marketplace in a broad spectrum of industries to speak to their employees. The First Wednesdays Forums provide valuable connections and novel perspectives. Belton says that the learning and the opportunity to make new partnerships and alliances are essential to keep the creative juices flowing. Addicks and others use First Wednesdays to visit other innovative companies, too. These opportunities foster innovation because you become more aware of fresh ideas that are emerging elsewhere. You say to yourself, "If they know that, we better know that, too."

Addicks and Belton shared ways that pausing to ask big questions with their teams brought about enormous growth and transformational innovation. They distilled three valuable pause moments:

1. *Backwards Pause.* Stepping back when things are not working in order to analyze how to take a new path
2. *Mission Pause.* Stepping back when we have lost our way and need to restore a sense of purpose
3. *Forward Pause.* Stepping back to envision aspirational dreams for imagining a big or a new possibility

Elaborating on "mission pause," Addicks and Belton told us that their first time working together was on Cheerios®. Along with their team, they stepped back to rethink and reposition the brand by more deeply considering how to engage the consumer. They asked, "What is the brand really about? How do we genuinely engage the consumer? What worked in the past? What hadn't worked?" Pausing to ask those questions and examining the history of their advertising helped them to realize that Cheerios is essentially about nurturing . . . someone nurturing someone else. What did they learn from this pause? When innovation aligns with deeper purpose and engagement, it goes to the heart of purpose for the consumer. Their exploration and discovery helped them to transform the brand by more deeply considering how they engage their customers.

Another important shift that took place internally for the General Mills team while reimagining the brand and analysis of the advertising was that everyone dropped their defenses once they realized that what they had done wasn't being critiqued. When it was clear that the objectives of the discussion were about learning and educating, the discussion and the value were elevated. They were open, and once they had the "DNA on the brand"—nurturing—everyone was aligned with this higher purpose.

Sharing an example of a "forward pause," they pointed to "The Future Now 2020" initiative, which is based on the idea that what is going to be happening in the future is already happening in small ways right now. Belton, Addicks, and their teams are pausing to ask, "What if we could see what's going to be happening in 2020, and what if we worked on them now?" They spent time visioning how they can be prepared. To pursue these questions, they are engaging in another kind of pause, bringing in people who can be catalysts for new thinking. They are looking at how to go to market and create new capabilities, which has resulted in a suite of new resources, including a database of highly engaged parents, multicultural marketing, and a digital ecosystem. They started looking at things differently, so they could say, "Let's make the future now."

MISSIONS TO MOVE
INNOVATION

Berrett-Koehler Publishers is a living example of an authentic, innovative culture that creates sustained value. Its founder and president, Steve Piersanti, is a humble yet confident and tenacious leader with strong convictions; he grounds the company and every decision that it makes, in their mission: "Creating a world that works for all." Its business model from the outset was extraordinarily innovative in the publishing world. In its twenty years, during the dramatic changes in the publishing industry, including the acquisitions of giant companies gobbling up others, recessions, and the introduction of digital book formats, Berrett-Koehler has been on the leading edge. It has had continuous growth and profitability while it has remained steadfast to its mission.

Founded on a commitment of social responsibility, Berrett-Koehler is always trying to serve all of its stakeholders, not only its investors and shareholders, but also its authors, suppliers, service providers, employees, customers, and extended community. To this end, they have a range of people, who represent all these groups, on their board. They have a Bill of Rights and Responsibilities that expresses the mutual partnership between the publisher and the author. Everything is transparent, and there is always a conscious interplay between service and accountability.

Steve Piersanti, a big believer in the value of pause, builds pauses intentionally into his life personally and professionally. Since prayer is his primary pause practice, he often works from his home office. He confesses that he's "worn out the knees of many pairs of pants." Another way that he pauses is by writing. It forces him to be more reflective, think about how he wants to respond to issues. He likes to gather a lot of information. When he has enough or is in a position where he needs to make a decision, he goes through all he has gathered, writes notes, and reflects. To bring pause to the Berrett-Koehler culture, Piersanti instituted a moment of silence before every staff meeting, giving everyone a chance to step back in their own way. For Steve, regular staff and management meetings are not just formality;

they are another way to structure pause into the life of the organization by scheduling time to thoughtfully review all aspects of the company's business. This forces him and others to stop what they are doing and devote time to preparing for such reviews. Pausing is the underlying catalyst for clarity, perspective, and innovation. Like many people, Steve says he gets some of his best breakthroughs when he is commuting on the bus or during the 10- or 15-minute walk from the bus to the office or his home. When we asked him how Berrett-Koehler had managed to be on the cutting edge of digital books, he said that it all started with pausing early, by having regular meetings with a diverse group of people who were willing to learn about the technology and determine how Berrett-Koehler would engage in this new frontier.

When Steve Piersanti decided to establish Berrett-Koehler based on a new and different model, a stewardship model, the language of stewardship set the tone for the culture of the company. He said, "When you are a steward, you are a trustee, and when you are a trustee you have a sense of responsibility for what you are entrusted with. When we talked to Steve about this, he reminded us, "When you choose the context of stewardship, the language of the model influences your entire perception from how you make decisions about what books to publish to how you regard all the stakeholders." Stewardship brings people together around a common purpose and a spirit of innovation generated by an intense desire to serve in new ways.

THE INNOVATIVE POWER OF WHY

Rohinish Hooda is vice president of U.S. sales and marketing, Ethicon Biosurgery, Johnson & Johnson. He is a "pause and think" guy who highly values the question, "Why?" From Rohinish's point of view, companies are hotbeds of hyperactivity, but too often they are not hotbeds of transformative thinking. He suggests that we give excessive attention and energy to filling up our calendars and to-do lists. We ask, "How can we get it done? When can we get it done?" But we need to ask, "Why are we doing it?"

Rohinish insists that curiosity is the key to creative thinking and to innovation. We need to ask questions, especially the "Why?" question, and we need to pause to answer it. As a leader, Rohinish drives his people to think about what they are doing and why. He values their insights. If we stop to ask "Why?" and answer the question, we create the opportunity for innovation.

Rohinish does not consider himself an innovator but a "provocateur" and an "enabler of innovation." Rohinish says that most new ideas come from others inside and outside his organization. He tries to value them, cultivate them by asking questions, incessantly prodding and encouraging them to crystallize their insights. "The results," he says, "are phenomenal solutions, that arise from getting everyone to stop and think."

BIG is a new innovation initiated by Rohinish. It stands for Bio Surgery Idea Gurus. This is his version of what Dyer, Gregersen, and Christensen call "TED in the head" or "The Medici Effect," coined by Frans Johansson, which is about the emergence of creativity that comes from intersecting cross-disciplinary ideas. Rohinish is dedicated to creating intersections of ideas by bringing brilliant, talented, passionate people together —surgeons, customers, employees— in small groups to talk about everything from new technologies and customer care to better outcomes, education, and new platforms. Rohinish Hooda provokes thinking by always asking the questions, "Why?" "What if?" "Why do you use these tools? Why make an incision this way? What if you had a different tool?" Then, he gathers the insights. He envisions BIG as the first of many cross-disciplinary groups that help break down silos, ignite new thinking by intersecting ideas, broadening perspectives, and seeing things from different points of view. Rohinish will share learning with other teams, challenge the status quo, experiment with new ideas, gather feedback, and evaluate the body of information. Then, Rohinish envisions taking the ideas to others to explore the potential impact and determine how to best advocate for them. Every step of the way, they pause to ask and answer the key questions: "Why?" "Why not?" "What if we did it another way?"

Breaking through Boundaries to Innovation

Jeannine McGlade and Andrew Pek, authors of the book *Stimulated!* and co-creators of iVibe Global, specialize in helping individuals and organizations grow by sparking creativity and shaping more innovative cultures. Jeannine and Andrew are conscious, continuous innovators. Personally, they pause to escape the everyday distractions of life, to turn down the noise and at least some of the technology, to sit and be quiet . . . to find stillness and to write. When working with organizations, they help others to pause to "awaken, stimulate, cultivate, harvest, and sustain" their creativity. They know well that creativity and innovation are an ongoing process of observation, exploration, and discovery that requires openness and connection to a meaningful purpose.

One of their biggest challenges is working with unyieldingly entrenched people. In one project, they were working with an animal health company, a division of a life sciences company that researches, develops, and manufactures feed additives, medicines, and other health care products for the safe, effective, and healthy growth of animals. While assessing the project, they learned that no one on the senior team had ever been to feed lots, dairy farms, or other constituents associated with their supply chain. They determined that taking the team to these environments to collect data and to have the experience of observational research could be a game changer. They also felt that the joint experience would be something that the team might bond around. Jeannine and Andrew did some training up front on techniques for observation. The dairy farm was their first field trip. Two people in the group were very resistant and negative. They were skeptical that a plan for innovation, especially one created by outside consultants, could be successful, and they had no interest in a field trip to a farm. "It did not fit their paradigm." They did go, however, and once there, resistance melted away; everyone, including the skeptics, became engaged. "The experience changed their frame of reference, perspective, and raised their consciousness. Once conscious and aware, you see things you never saw before. It was like an anthropological dig. It shifted their thinking. They became more deeply connected to their purpose, had renewed energy, and were open to seeing things in a new way." Jeannine and Andrew characterize the observational research as "a reflective, pause-oriented activity that sparked creative thinking and energy in an otherwise stuck senior team."

Jeannine and Andrew said that their biggest challenge of all is when senior leaders think pausing to think in new ways is for everyone else, but not for them. Ideally, they work with the senior leader and all key leaders. They call this "training a network of champions." Their work to initiate innovative growth includes the underlying conditions to support it, which can include new ways to connect with and engage customers, ways to innovate the workplace environment, and the development of metrics . . . everything needed to support the intention. "We're no longer needed when the new processes and behaviors become embodied in the organization and they take on a life of their own. We have succeeded when we help the organization become commercially successful, socially relevant, and making a difference in people's lives."

Balancing Immediate Drive with Future Innovation

The generics pharmaceutical industry is a fast-paced, "deliver-it-now," continuously changing business landscape. The immediacy of results makes it an easy place to get caught up in the here-and-now, hyperactive drive for results. However, if you do not have a long-term view of talent and innovation, competition will overtake you quickly.

Jeff George, global head of Sandoz, was recently listed as number nine in *Fortune* magazine's "40 under 40," along with Facebook's Mark Zuckerberg and Google's Larry Page. Jeff's fast-paced, results-driven, lightning-quick approaches fit the generics industry well. Like other strong leaders, he has developed complementary strengths to balance and focus his drive. Jeff has an extraordinary ability to create passionate, purposeful, connected cultures that are driven and innovative. He has transformed Sandoz from the traditional generics culture to a dynamic, highly desirable, highly sought after culture—"a place to be"—for global talent. Jeff goes out of his way to recruit, develop, acknowledge, and appreciate his talent. He is not afraid to show his emotions publicly and demonstrate his care for people, sometimes to the point of a tinge of embarrassment or discomfort. Interviewing his team, I discovered that each person felt being a part of this team was by far the best experience of their careers. Jeff George drives business results because he creates a great culture.

Jeff gets some of his balance by meditating each morning to renew awareness and clarity about himself and his intentions for the day. Commenting on his pause practice, he said, "My meditation practice gives me the ability to pause deeply within myself as a preparation for the day. I tend to be energetic and driven. The meditation helps me to bring my whole self—drive and heart, passion and purpose—to all that I do and into all my interactions with my teams. Leaders must step back to drive forward with both heart and mind."

Shifting Focus and Opening Up Possibilities

Pause is the fundamental growth process by which we can move from management effectiveness to leadership innovation. Pause liberates us from the imprisonment of the reactive "stimulus/response" pattern of non-agile management and frees us to proactively cultivate the possibilities that derive from the "stimulus/pause/multiple responses" of curious, learning-agile leadership.

Pause is the human mechanism that allows us to break the reactive boundaries of our past conditioning to the creative, innovative, multifaceted repertoire of first-time breakthroughs. Pause provides multiple potential futures, multiple possibilities for innovative leadership.

Robert was an extremely bright and effective CEO of a multibillion-dollar consumer products company. Always two or three steps ahead of his team, his quick mind could solve most problems. However, during a severe financial crisis, he and his team hit the wall. Tried and true solutions just looked old and tired. Nothing seemed to be an optimal strategic way out. Overwhelmed by the complexity, uncertainty, and many variables that made it feel impossible to use history to predict the future, Robert's team was drained. His run of uninterrupted successes in the past compelled him to keep pushing for what had always worked, yet nothing was working. Finally, he and his team found the courage and the wisdom to step back and look at themselves and their marketplace with fresh eyes. They studied successful companies outside of their industry. They visited Google, Apple, Salesforce.com, and Procter & Gamble. They invited consultants from different industries to share expertise with them. They assessed and coached themselves to step up as more effective, innovative leaders. They recruited people who came from different industries and had radically different experience from them, and they welcomed the diversity. They learned to see the novel and different ideas presented by their talent as creative tension that catalyzed learning. They pressed themselves to have a breakthrough strategy, not an incremental one. They questioned more, reflected more, and synthesized new perspectives. As Robert and the team engaged and paused for their individual, team, and strategic growth, their new strategy, culture, and mission became clearer. Commenting on the transformation, Robert shared with me, "It all started with stepping back. If we had just worked harder and harder with our same approaches, we may have survived, but we would never have made the innovative breakthrough." Innovation begins with an agile leader who proactively engages others in the shift to a new reality.

Managers move the current organization into the future, whereas leaders transcend current realities to create the future now.

Step Back to Lead Forward: Seven Pause Practices to Grow Cultures of Innovation

Consider growing an enduring, value-creating culture of innovation by using these seven crucial, powerful pause practices:

Pause to Grow Innovation Practice 1: Be On-Purpose

Take the time to clarify your motivating values and compelling purpose, individually and collectively. Purpose fuels energy and drive to go beyond what is, and it continues until something extraordinary has been created. Purpose is the value-creating, energy-multiplying life force of innovation.

Pause to Grow Innovation Practice 2: Question and Listen

Step back to be open and curious by using the language of innovation: questioning and listening. Strive to ask the extra question to challenge yourself and others to go deeper and stretch further. Hone your questioning and listening skills to activate your collective innovation potential. Seek out diverse viewpoints to observe problems or opportunities from a fresh point of view. *Managers leap to the answers; leaders trust curiosity, and the learning that results from inquiry.*

Pause to Grow Innovation Practice 3: Risk Experimentation

Have the courage to accelerate through failure by building momentum and speed through new learning. Experimentation steers us to our eventual destination through its roadblocks, twists, and turns, as long as we are learning agile and courageous enough to persist. Step back to make sure your behaviors, as well as your systems and processes, are not unduly restricting the risk of experimentation. Make sure your key people are encouraged to spend at least 15 percent of their time exploring and prototyping new ideas.

Pause to Grow Innovation Practice 4: Reflect and Synthesize

Set aside time, in the manner that works for you, for integration and synthesis. A CFO of a major company sets aside every Sunday evening to mind map his most complex or strategic issues. He gets all pieces laid out and then begins to link them up by associating the divergent parts into a more integrated whole. Identify your best way to daily or weekly "cut through the clutter" to gain clarity and new possibility.

Pause to Grow Innovation Practice 5: Consider Inside-Out and Outside-In Dynamics

Step back to consider the forces shaping the future by looking at both internal and external cues. Foster optimal creativity internally and consider competitive, global, and futuristic dynamics in an integrated manner. Transformative innovation stands at the crossroads of internal, collaborative creativity and external, customer-focused needs.

Pause to Grow Innovation Practice 6: Foster Generativity

Take the time to connect, coach, mentor, and develop your people. Constructively challenge their thinking, strategy, and behavior through the lens of innovation. Stretch people to create, to innovate, and to envision alternative futures. Grow your people to grow a culture of innovation.

Pause to Grow Innovation Practice 7: Be Authentic

The innovation potential of your teams or organization will be directly proportional to your innovation embodiment. Make sure your behaviors are not unknowingly limiting a culture of innovation. Ask for feedback. "How could I encourage even more innovation here?" Most important, be the innovator you wish to see in your culture.

PAUSE POINT:
VISIONING A CULTURE OF INNOVATION

Imagine your organization comprised of leaders continually striving to authentically bring their best to every endeavor. Your team is open, collaborative, and engaged. Your key talent has the skills and experience to stretch your organization into the future. Your organization is focused on a purposeful, meaningful mission that compels everyone to serve and stretch beyond the status quo. Ask yourself:

- What would be possible for your team and organization?

- What could be created by your team and organization?

o What would be required of you and your team to create this culture of continuous growth and innovation?

o What can you do to begin this now?

THREE AFTER WORDS:
PAUSE IT FORWARD . . .

I hope our journey together has been helpful and meaningful as we explored the growth regions of self, others, and innovation. However, there are much bigger pauses to take, much deeper reflections to make. Pause to tackle big, complex, global issues so multifaceted and multidimensional that only a collective group of enlightened leaders could get their arms around them.

What if a critical mass of leaders paused not only to influence their immediate concerns but also stepped back for a bigger transformation . . . the transformation of the toughest issues we face as citizens in a global society? What if a tipping point of leaders rallied around the purposeful aspiration to pause and to act on the really significant, complex issues we all face? Signs of such major, service-fueled, purpose-filled initiatives are cropping up and making progress. The Clinton Health Access Initiative is making health care available to people in Africa. The Bill & Melinda Gates Foundation is intent on eradicating entire classes of disease. The Climate Reality Project is educating and galvanizing awareness and changes to stem issues of climate change. Habitat for Humanity has rallied communities to build more than 500,000 safe, affordable homes. Berkana Institute approaches seemingly insurmountable problems in new ways, and for more than two decades Margaret Wheatley, its founder, has been teaching others to discover new approaches in our chaotic world. Jane McGonigal, the world-renowned alternate reality game designer, founded Gameful to inspire and challenge innovative game designers to design games that will improve people's lives and solve real problems. She believes that in the future a game designer could be a Nobel Peace Prize winner. The Presencing Institute, a global community of individuals, institutions, and leaders, are transforming lives and communities by creating new models to deal with the issues of hunger, water, illiteracy, and poverty. Paul Polak, founder of International Development Enterprises, is developing practical solutions that attack poverty at its roots. Like Wheatley, Senge, Scharmer, and others, Polak implores us to listen to the people living in these situations and learn as much as we can about them and the context in which they live. All these initiatives and countless others are examples of stepping back to lead forward with enduring, innovative, life-enhancing impact.

As you are about to finish this book, I encourage you to pause for two very important final reflections:

1. *Pause It Now.* First and foremost, are you doing everything possible to grow yourself, grow others, and grow innovation? Global transformation begins with leaders like you authentically serving their immediate spheres of influence.

2. *Pause It Forward.* Second, what more could you also do to "play a bigger game" to more positively influence the broader systems and human needs in our local communities and the world?

For years, my "bigger game" has been to help influence the character development of hundreds of thousands of school-aged children through my association with Youth Frontiers. Also, my senior fellow and board memberships with the Caux Roundtable and the Center for Ethical Business Cultures are my attempt to foster ethical transformations in CEO leadership. Working at both ends of the age spectrum, from the young leaders of the future to today's seasoned leaders, supplements the work that I do daily with my leadership clients and contributes to my larger, more generative purpose. This is my small, but I hope significant, way to pause it forward. What is yours?

If we each step back to consider how to do our part, we may have a chance to lead forward to foster more enriching, sustaining futures for successive generations. As Ray Anderson said, "Unless someone leads no one will." It is up to us, the current generation of leaders, to create the future. It is up to us to pause it forward with authenticity, purpose, and generativity.

Great space has no corners.
Great talent ripens late.
Great eloquence is silent.
Great form is shapeless.
The subtle essence of the universe is hidden and
indefinable, yet its benefit is always bestowed.

—Lao-Tzu

NOTES

This book draws on our learning and experience working with leaders for more than three decades and interviews conducted for this book. In some cases, individuals preferred that we exclude their names and business names. For all others, we cited them and our conversations in the text.

I took the liberty of updating the wording of Chuang Tzu's quote in the front of the book with no intention of changing the meaning. The original quote reads: "To act with the minimum of effort and obtain the maximum results, such is the way of the wise leader."

Chapter One: Introducing the Pause Principle

"VUCA world" was introduced by the Army War College and by Bob Johansen in his book, *Get There Early* (San Francisco: Berrett-Koehler, 2007), pages 45–46.

The reference to Daniel Kahneman and his work identifying two systems of thinking comes from *Time*, December 15, 2011, page 1, www.time. com/time/magazine/article/0,9171,2099712,00.html. To read more, see Daniel Kahneman, *Thinking, Fast and Slow* (New York: Farrar, Straus and Giroux, 2011). The comment on what scientists know about creativity and "Aha!" moments was made by Dr. Erick Kandel, Charlie Rose Brain Series 2, *Consciousness*, December 5, 2011. Jonah Lehrer's remarks were extracted from an interview published online by Barnes & Noble, March 27, 2012, pages 1–5. http://bnreview.barnesandnoble.com/t5/Interview/quot-The-residue-of-time-wasted-quot-Jonah-Lehrer-Talks/ba-p/7283.

Neal Maillet, Berrett-Koehler editorial director, brought to our attention the valuable research by Barton and Sutcliffe. Michelle A. Barton and Kathleen M. Sutcliffe, "Learning to Stop Momentum," *MIT Sloan Management Review*, Vol. 51, no. 3 (Spring 2010), pages 69–76.

A reference to a "pause moment" was made by Richard Leider, *The Power of Purpose* (San Francisco: Berrett-Koehler, 2010), page 3. During our interview, Leider cited his annual expedition to Africa as a big pause. The reference to an article on the need for more space was by David Allen, "When Technology Overwhelms, It's Time to Get Organized," *New York Times*, March 18, 2012, SR pages 1 and 4. The Theory U/Presencing concepts are from the book, C. Otto Scharmer, *Theory U* (San Francisco: Berrett-Koehler, 2011), pages 31–34. Scharmer references a discussion he and Joseph Jaworski had with W. Brian Arthur about changing economic foundations. Arthur discusses two levels of cognition or "knowing." An excellent article on how executive careers plateau if they do not develop interpersonal skills and other higher-order competencies and strategies is Kenneth R. Brousseau, Michael J. Driver, Gary Hourihan, and Rikard Larsson, "The Seasoned Executive's Decision-Making Style," *Harvard Business Review* (February 2006). All the examples of pragmatic pause come from our interviews.

We first heard about São Paulo's ban on print advertising in the 2011 documentary/comedy by Morgan Spurlock and Jeremy Chilnick, *The Greatest Movie Ever Sold*. Curious, we explored online sources, including "Billboard Ban in São Paulo Angers Advertisers," *New York Times*, December 12, 2006, www.nytimes.com/2006/12/12/world/americas/12iht-brazil.html, and Patrick Burgoyne, "São Paulo: The City That Said No to Advertising," *Businessweek*, www.businessweek.com/innovate/content/jun2007/id20070 618_505580.htm.

During our interview with Dr. Thomas Morgan, Augsburg College, he referred us to Eric E. Vogt, Juanita Brown, and David Isaacs, *The Art of Powerful Questions* (Mill Valley, CA: Whole Systems Associates, 2003), pages 2 and 1. We found that the significance of continuous questioning bears out in the research on innovators by Jeff Dyer, Hal Gregersen, and Clayton Christensen, *The Innovator's DNA* (Boston: Harvard Business Review Press, 2011), pages 23–40.

During the final weeks of writing the manuscript, we had the privilege of reading part of Paul Laudicina's new book in draft form and discussing it with him. To read more, look for Paul Laudicina, *Beating the Global Odds* (New York: Wiley, 2012). For research on the demand for leaders who can deal with ambiguity and complex challenges, see M. M. Lombardo and R. W. Eichinger, *The Leadership Machine*, researched by Lominger International (Minneapolis: Lominger International, 2001). Center for Creative Leadership research presented at Conference Board Executive Coaching Conference, February 2008.

Terry Bacon, my colleague, has researched and written extensively on power and influence. In a conversation, we talked about drive and credibility. For more on aspects of influence, see Terry Bacon, *The Elements of Influence* (New York: AMACOM, 2011).

I had the privilege of meeting and talking with Warren Bennis. The following book and his other writings have been important influences. Warren Bennis, *On Becoming a Leader* (Reading, MA: Addison-Wesley, 1990).

Chapter Two: Pause to Grow Personal Leadership

The research referenced on the relationship between self-awareness and successful leadership comes from: J. P. Flaum, "When It Comes to Business Leadership, Nice Guys Finish First," Green Peak Partners, pages 4 and 6. The article was based on the study, "What Predicts Executive Success," done in collaboration with Cornell University. The article on managerial self-awareness is Allan H. Church and W. Warner Burke Associates, "Managerial Self-Awareness in High-Performing Individuals in Organizations," *Journal of Applied Psychology*, Vol. 82, no. 2 (1997), pages 281–92. To read more on the research basis for self-awareness, see Daniel Goleman, *Emotional Intelligence* (New York: Bantam, 1995); Jim Collins, *Good to Great* (New York: HarperCollins, 2001); John H. Zenger and Joseph Folkman, *The Extraordinary Leader* (New York: McGraw-Hill, 2002). The reference to "three abilities" comes from an interview with Daniel Goleman by Dan Schawbel, "Daniel Goleman on Leadership and The Power of Emotional Intelligence," *Forbes*, page 2. Additional references supporting whole-person development: Daniel Goleman, *Working with Emotional Intelligence* (New York: Bantam, 1998), pages 26–27. Daniel Goleman, Richard Boyatzis, and Annie McKee, *Primal Leadership* (Boston: Harvard Business School Press, 2004), page 94. The quote by Bill George is from: Bill George, *True North* (San Francisco: Jossey-Bass, 2007), page 65. The full reference to Brooks's brilliant book is David Brooks, *The Social Animal: The Hidden Sources of Love, Character and Achievement* (New York: Random House, 2011), pages 39 and 45.

Emerson's essay, "Character," is available in various collections. One source is Brooks Atkinson, *The Essential Writings of Ralph Waldo Emerson* (New York: Modern Library, 2000), pages 327–40. For more on "The Study of Character," see the work by Terry Bacon, *The Elements of Power* (New York: AMACOM, 2011), pages 3, 127, 115–119. The reference to Hamlet is in Act IV, Scene V, William Shakespeare, *Hamlet* (New York: Simon & Schuster, 1958). Our source for the description of the Character Foundation Assessment™ is Grant Peirce, The Peirce Group. Someone sent me the "thousand tiny surrenders . . ." quote. The author gave us permission to use it but preferred not to be identified because we extracted it from its fuller context.

Insights about Steve Jobs through interviews from people who knew him and especially by Walter Isaacson were enlightening. For a more complete understanding, read: Walter Isaacson, *Steve Jobs* (New York: Simon & Schuster, 2011). The reference to Howard Schultz's comments on purpose come from an online interview: Gagen Mac Donald, "Connecting with Purpose and Meaning," *Let Go & Lead Series Four*, conversation with Howard Schultz; www.letgoandlead.com/2011/08/howard-schultz-connecting-with-purpose-meaning/.

Reference to the benefits of walking and taking a nap are from "31 Ways to Get Smarter Faster," *Newsweek*, January 9, 2012, page 29. Another source on the beneficial connection between sleep and innovation is Jeff Dyer, Hal Gregersen, and Clayton Christensen, *The Innovator's DNA* (Boston: Harvard Business Review Press, 2011), page 57.

Walter Isaacson's biography on Albert Einstein is fascinating. Walter Isaacson, *Einstein* (New York: Simon & Schuster, 2009), pages 113–33. The reference to the important connection Steve Jobs made between his knowledge of calligraphy and the creation of fonts is a widely told story, one he related in his speech to graduates of Stanford University. For the text, see the following link: http://news.stanford.edu/news/2005/june15/jobs-061505.html.

Reference to research on meditation showing improvements in brain activity and intelligence, as well as metabolic functions, include M. C. Dillbeck et al., "Frontal EEG Coherence, H-Reflex Recovery, Concept Learning, and the TM-Sidhi Program," *International Journal of Neuroscience* Vol. 15 (1981), pages 151–57; M. C. Dillbeck, "Meditation and Flexibility of Visual Perception and Verbal Problem-Solving," *Memory & Cognition* 10, (1982), pages 207–15. M. C. Dillbeck et al., "Longitudinal Effects of the Transcendental Meditation and TM-Sidhi Program on Cognitive Ability and Cognitive Style," *Perceptual and Motor Skills* 62 (1986), pages 731–38. S. Yamamoto et al., "Medial Prefrontal Cortex and Anterior Cingulated Cortex in the Generation of Alpha Activity Induced by Transcendental Meditation: A Magnetoencephalographic Study," *Acta Medica Okayama* Vol. 60, no. 1 (2006), pages 51–58. J. Anderson et al., "Blood Pressure Response to Transcendental Meditation: A Meta-analysis," *American Journal of Hypertension* Vol. 21, no. 3 (2008), pages 310–16. V. A. Barnes et al., "Stress, Stress Reduction, and Hypertension in African Americans," *Journal of the National Medical Association* Vol. 89 (1997), pages 464–76.

To see considerable research on the benefits of mindfulness meditation and other mindfulness practices, go to University of Massachusetts, Center for Mindfulness in Medicine, Health Care, and Society, www.umassmed.edu/Content.aspx?id=42426. The reference to the PBS, *Healing and the Mind* program can be found in Bill Moyers, *Healing and the Mind* (New York: Doubleday, 1993), pages 122–23.

To read more about Maslow and his work on peak experiences and Csikszentimihalyi's work on flow, see Abraham Maslow, *Toward a*

Psychology of Being (New York: Van Nostrand-Rheinhold, 1968), or Mihaly Csikszentimihalyi, *Flow* (New York: Harper Perennial, 1991). For more on presencing, we recommend C. Otto Scharmer, *Theory U* (San Francisco: Berrett-Koehler, 2009), pages 8, 29–30, 38–47, 49–52; Peter Senge, C. Otto Scharmer, Joseph Jaworski, and Betty Sue Flowers, *Presence* (New York: Doubleday, 2004), pages 13–15, 213–34.

Kabat-Zinn's quote on "the interior landscape" is from Jon Kabat-Zinn, *Coming to Our Senses* (New York: Hyperion, 2006), page 23.

References to the modern whole-brain theory and intelligent memory are from William Duggan, "How Aha! Really Happens," *strategy+business*, no. 61 (November 23, 2010), pages 1–2. Additional references he cites are B. Milner, L. R. Squire, E. R. Kandel, *Neuron*, Vol. 20, no. 3 (March 1998), pages 445–68; Barry Gordon and Lisa Berger, *Intelligent Memory* (New York: Viking, 2003); Timothy Wilson, *Strangers to Ourselves* (Cambridge, MA: Harvard University Press, 2002), pages 6 and 24. References to the conscious and unconscious mind come from Charlie Rose Brain Series 2, *Consciousness*, December 5, 2011. For Daniel Pink's reference to Betty Edwards's insight about drawing, see Daniel Pink, *A Whole New Mind* (New York: Penguin, 2005), page 15.

Chapter Three: Pause to Grow Others

Ram Charan has made significant contributions to our understanding of business strategy and the importance of identifying and developing talent for organizational growth and contribution. Ram Charan and Bill Conaty, *The Talent Masters* (New York: Crown, 2010), page 1.

For more on Level V Leaders, read Jim Collins, *Good to Great* (New York: Harper Collins, 2001), pages 25–40.

In 1997, we attended a spectacular exhibit of Dale Chihuly's glass sculptures at the Minneapolis Institute of Art. We were as impressed with the videos and writing on his team process and the abundance mentality that is a part of it as we were with the exceptional pieces on exhibit. To learn more, go to Dale Chihuly's website, www.chihuly.com/chihuly-biography. aspx, Writings about the Artist.

To see the research supporting the business case for developing leaders, go to Corporate Executive Board, "A Senior Leader's Guide to Leader-Led Development: Understanding Your Role in the Nest Generation of Leaders" (Washington, DC: Corporate Executive Board, 2007), page 6.

For more on the significance of questions, see Eric Vogt, Juanita Brown, and David Isaacs, *The Art of Powerful Questions* (Mill Valley, CA: Whole Systems Associates, 2003), page 1. Jeff Dyer, Hal Gregersen, and Clayton Christensen, *The Innovator's DNA* (Boston: Harvard Business Review Press, 2011), pages 23 and 65–88.

The listening research is eye opening. To read more, go to Kelly E. See, Elizabeth Wolfe Morrison, Naomi B. Rothman, and Jack B. Soll, "The Detrimental Effects of Power on Confidence, Advice Taking, and Accuracy," *Organizational Behavior and Human Decision Processes* (2011), pages 1–12. Steve Nguyen, "Bosses and Powerful People Do Not Listen," *Workplace Psychology* (2011), http://workplacepsychology .net/?s=Bosses+and+Powerful +People+Do+Not+Listen.

Michelle A. Barton and Kathleen M. Sutcliffe, "Learning to Stop Momentum," *MIT Sloan Management Review*, Vol. 51, no. 3 (Spring 2010), pages 71–76. We heard Peter Senge's "eye of the needle" story in his audiobook: Peter Senge, *The Power of Presence* (Sounds True, 2008). The insight by Senge is from Peter Senge, *The Fifth Discipline Fieldbook* (New York: Crown, 1994). The op-ed piece by Thomas Friedman, "Help Wanted," *New York Times*, December 18, 2011, pages 1–3, includes the quotes by Dov Seidman. Noel Tichy and Warren Bennis, "Wise Leaders Cultivate Two Traits," *Leadership Excellence* (June 2007), page 3. Daniel Coyle, *The Talent Code* (New York: Bantam, 2009), pages 32–33, 38–45, 44, and 18.

For more on the Novartis case study, see the whitepaper: Kevin Cashman, Janet Feldman, Katie Cooney, and George Hallenbeck, "Accelerated Leadership Development and Succession: Korn/Ferry's Impact at Novartis" (Korn/Ferry Institute, 2010), pages 1–7. It is available at www.Cashman Leadership.com.

To read more on generativity and the other life cycle stages, see Erik H. Erikson and Joan M. Erikson, *The Life Cycle Complete* (New York: Norton, 1997), pages 55–109.

Chapter Four: Pause to Grow Cultures of Innovation

The description by Banesh Hoffman of Albert Einstein was translated from a Spanish edition of *Einstein* by Banesh Hoffman (Editorial Salvat de Grandes Biografías). The other references to Einstein come from Walter Isaacson, *Einstein* (New York: Simon & Schuster, 2009), pages 113–33; Walter Isaacson, *American Sketches* (New York: Simon & Schuster, 2009), pages 129, 143–45. Walter Isaacson's statement about the similarities between Albert Einstein and Steve Jobs are from a live interview Isaacson did with Charlie Rose after Steve Jobs's death in October 2011.

Otto Scharmer's *Theory U* is a comprehensive, pragmatic approach for fostering new thinking and innovative solutions. C. Otto Scharmer, *Theory U* (San Francisco: Berrett-Koehler, 2009), pages 22, 15, 17, and 14.

Sources for Ray Anderson and Interface, Inc.: Ray Anderson with Robin White, *Confessions of a Radical Industrialist* (New York: St. Martin's Press, 2009); Ray Anderson, *A Call for Systemic Change* (Population Press, 2004), www.populationpress.org/publication/2004-2-anderson.html. Retrieved January 3, 2012. Ray Anderson, on the business logic of sustainability, TED, February 2009, www.ted.com/talks/ray_anderson_on_the_business_logic_of_sustainability .html. TED refers to Technology, Entertainment and Design. Talks are on topics that may have a positive influence on the world. For more about TED, to view talks or learn how to apply to give one, go to www.ted.com/. Interface website: History, Culture, Mission/Vision and Values: www.interfaceglobal. com/Sustainability/Interface-Story.aspx. Retrieved January 12, 2012. Editor, "Ray Anderson Leads Business Down a Sustainable Path," *Sustainable Living*, pages 1–3. Retrieved December 27, 2011, www.sustainablelivingmagazine .org/business/eco-business/74-ray-anderson-leads-the-way.

Jane Stevenson and Bilal Kaafarani, *Breaking Away* (New York: McGraw-Hill, 2011), pages 15–26.

Sources on Steve Piersanti and Berrett-Koehler Publishers are accessible on the Berrett-Koehler website, www.bkconnection.com. There is a video of Steve and links to feature articles, news, press releases, the Bill of Rights and Responsibilities, a discussion guide for Peter Block, *Stewardship* (San Francisco: Berrett-Koehler, 1998). Articles include "Taking a Page from Its Books," *Motto Media* (March/April 2007), pages 39–41. Lucas Conley, "Getting on the Same Page," *Fast Company.com*, November 1, 2005, pages 1–2. Hua-Ching Ni, *The Complete Works of Lao-Tzu* (Santa Monica, CA: Seven Star Communications, 1995), page 59. "TED in the head" comes from Jeff Dyer, Hal Gregersen, and Clayton Christensen, *The Innovator's DNA* (Boston: Harvard Business Review Press, 2011), page 47. The term "The Medici Effect" is from Frans Joseph, *The Medici Effect* (Boston: Harvard Business School Press, 2006), page 20.

BIBLIOGRAPHY

Allen, David. "When Technology Overwhelms, It's Time to Get Organized." *New York Times*, March 18, 2012, pp. SR1, SR 4.

Anderson, Ray, with Robin White. *Confessions of a Radical Industrialist: Profits, People, Purpose—Doing Business by Respecting the Earth.* New York: St. Martin's Press, 2009.

Bacon, Terry R. *The Elements of Influence: The Art of Getting Others to Follow Your Lead.* New York: AMACOM, 2011.

Bacon, Terry R. *The Elements of Power: Lessons on Leadership and Influence.* New York: AMACOM, 2011.

Barton, Michelle A., and Kathleen M. Sutcliffe. "Learning to Stop Momentum." *MIT Sloan Management Review* Vol. 51, no. 3 (Spring 2010): 69–76.

Bennis, Warren. *On Becoming a Leader* (Reading, MA: Addison-Wesley, 1990).

Block, Peter. *Stewardship: Choosing Service over Self-Interest.* San Francisco: Berrett-Koehler, 1996.

Brooks, David. *The Social Animal: The Hidden Sources of Love, Character, and Achievement.* New York: Random House, 2011.

Brousseau, Kenneth R., Michael J. Drive, Gary Hourihan, and Rikard Larsson. "The Seasoned Executive's Decision-Making Style." *Harvard Business Review* (February 2006): 111–21.

Brown, Juanita, with David Isaacs and the World Café Community. *The World Café: Shaping Our Futures through Conversations That Matter.* San Francisco: Berrett-Koehler, 2005.

Cashman, Kevin. *Awakening the Leader Within: A Story of Transformation.* Hoboken: NJ: John Wiley & Sons, 2003.

Cashman, Kevin. *Leadership from the Inside Out: Becoming a Leader for Life.* San Francisco: Berrett-Koehler, 2008.

Charan, Ram, and Bill Conaty. *The Talent Masters: Why Smart Leaders Put People before Numbers.* New York: Crown, 2010.

Christensen, Clayton M. *The Innovator's Dilemma: The Revolutionary Book That Will Change the Way You Do Business.* New York: HarperCollins, 2005.

Collins, Jim. *Good to Great: Why Some Companies Make the Leap . . . and Others Don't.* New York: Penguin, 2005.

Collins, Jim, and Jerry Porras. *Built to Last: Successful Habits of Visionary Companies.* New York: HarperCollins, 2004.

Corporate Executive Board, "A Senior Leader's Guide to Leader-Led Development: Understanding Your Role in the Next Generation of Leaders." Washington, DC: Corporate Executive Board, 2007.

Coyle, Daniel. *The Talent Code: Greatness Isn't Born. It's Grown. Here's How.* New York: Bantam, 2009.

Csikszentimihalyi, Mihaly. *Flow: The Psychology of Optimal Experience.* New York: Harper Perennial, 1991.

Dyer, Jeff, Hal Gregersen, and Clayton M. Christensen. *The Innovator's DNA: Mastering the Five Skills of Disruptive Innovators.* Boston: Harvard Business Review Press, 2011.

Einstein, Albert. *Einstein on Humanism: Collected Essays of Albert Einstein.* Secaucus, NJ: Carol Publishing, 1993.

Emerson, Ralph Waldo. *The Collected Works of Ralph Waldo Emerson.* Cambridge, MA: Harvard University Press, 1984.

Erikson, Erik H., and Joan M. Erikson. *The Life Cycle Completed: Extended Version with New Chapters on the Ninth Stage of Development.* New York: Norton, 1997.

George, Bill, with Peter Sims. *True North.* San Francisco: Jossey-Bass, 2007.

George, Bill, and Doug Baker. *True North Groups: A Powerful Path to Personal and Leadership Development.* San Francisco: Berrett-Koehler, 2011.

Goleman, Daniel. *Emotional Intelligence: Why It Can Matter More Than IQ.* New York: Bantam, 1994.

Goleman, Daniel. *Working with Emotional Intelligence.* New York: Bantam, 1998.

Isaacson, Walter. *American Sketches: Great Leaders, Creative Thinkers, and Heroes of a Hurricane.* New York: Simon & Schuster, 2009.

Isaacson, Walter. *Einstein: His Life and Universe.* New York: Simon & Schuster, 2009.

Isaacson, Walter. *Steve Jobs.* New York: Simon & Schuster, 2011.

Jaworski, Joseph. *Synchronicity: The Inner Path of Leadership.* San Francisco: Berrett-Koehler, 2011.

Johansen, Bob. *Get There Early: Sensing the Future to Compete in the Present.* San Francisco: Berrett-Koehler, 2007.

Johansen, Bob. *Leaders Make the Future: Ten New Leadership Skills for an Uncertain World.* San Francisco: Berrett-Koehler, 2009.

Johansson, Frans. *The Medici Effect: What Elephants and Epidemics Can Teach Us About Innovation.* Boston: Harvard Business School Press, 2006.

Jung, C. G. *Basic Writings of C. G. Jung.* New York: Random House, 1993.

Kabat-Zinn, Jon. *Coming to Our Senses: Healing Ourselves and the World through Mindfulness.* New York: Hyperion, 2005.

Kabat-Zinn, Jon. *Full Catastrophe Living: Using the Wisdom of Your Body and Mind to Face Stress, Pain, and Illness.* New York: Bantam Dell, 2005.

Kahneman, Daniel. *Thinking, Fast and Slow.* New York: Farrar, Straus and Giroux, 2011.

Kelley, Tom with Jonathan Littman. *The Ten Faces of Innovation: IDEO's Strategies for Beating the Devil's Advocate and Driving Creativity throughout Your Organization.* New York: Doubleday, 2005.

Laudicina, Paul. *Beating the Global Odds: High Stakes Decision Making for Success.* New York: Wiley, 2012.

Lehrer, Jonah. *Imagine: How Creativity Works.* Boston: Houghton Mifflin Harcourt, 2012.

Leider, Richard. *The Power of Purpose: Creating Meaning in Your Life and Work.* San Francisco: Berrett-Koehler, 2010.

Leider, Richard. *Repacking Your Bags: Lighten Your Load for the Rest of Your Life.* San Francisco: Berrett-Koehler, 2012.

Lombardo, M. M., and R. W. Eichinger. *The Leadership Machine.* Minneapolis: Lominger International, 2001.

Maslow, Abraham. *Toward a Psychology of Being.* New York: Van Nostrand-Rheinhold, 1968.

Melrose, Ken. *Making the Grass Greener on Your Side.* San Francisco: Berrett-Koehler, 1995.

Moyers, Bill. *Healing and the Mind.* New York: Doubleday, 1993.

Pek, Andrew, and Jeannine McGlade. *Stimulated!* Austin, TX: Greenleaf Book Group Press, 2008.

Pink, Daniel. *A Whole New Mind: Moving from the Information Age to the Conceptual Age.* New York: Penguin, 2005.

Scharmer, C. Otto. *Theory U: Leading from the Future as It Emerges.* San Francisco: Berrett-Koehler, 2009.

See, Kelly E., Elizabeth Wolfe Morrison, Naomi B. Rothman, and Jack B. Soll. "The Detrimental Effects of Power on Confidence, Advice Taking, and Accuracy." *Organizational Behavior and Human Decision Processes* (2011): 1–12.

Seidman, Dov. *How: Why How We Do Anything Means Everything . . . in Business (and in Life).* Hoboken, NJ: Wiley, 2007.

Senge, Peter M. *The Fifth Discipline: The Art and Practice of the Learning Organization.* New York: Doubleday Currency, 1994.

Senge, Peter, C. Otto Scharmer, Joseph Jaworski, and Betty Sue Flowers. *Presence: An Exploration of Profound Change in People, Organizations, and Society.* New York: Doubleday Currency, 2005.

Stevenson, Jane, and Bilal Kaafarani. *Breaking Away: How Great Leaders Create Innovation That Drives Sustainable Growth—and Why Others Fail.* New York: McGraw-Hill, 2011.

Tichy, Noel M., and Warren Bennis. *Judgment: How Winning Leaders Make Great Calls.* New York: Portfolio, 2007.

Vogt, Eric, Juanita Brown, and David Isaacs. "The Art of Powerful Questions: Catalyzing Insight, Innovation, and Action." Mill Valley, CA: Whole Systems Associates, 2003.

Wheatley, Margaret. *Leadership and the New Science: Discovering Order in a Chaotic World.* San Francisco: Berrett-Koehler, 1999.

Wilson, Timothy D. *Strangers to Ourselves: Discovering the Adaptive Unconscious.* Cambridge, MA: Harvard University Press, 2002.

Zenger, John H., and Joseph Folkman. *The Extraordinary Leader: Turning Good Managers into Great Leaders.* New York: McGraw-Hill, 2002.

ACKNOWLEDGMENTS

A new book is definitely an intense birthing process that involves contributions by many midwives, each of whom deserve a pause for heartfelt thanks.

First, my deepest gratitude is to Soraya, my spouse and spiritual soul mate. Your help, brainstorming, insightful feedback, and inspiring quotes kept me energized and enthused. The sacrifices you made to give me so much precious time to pause for this book, when I should have been pausing more with you, was a selfless, loving gift. Thank you for your love always.

Second, thanks to Margie Adler, my developmental editor. Without Margie, *The Pause Principle* would not exist. You were my creative partner, my patient collaborator, the energetic force that moved things forward. All authors should be so fortunate to have the incredible support of an editor like you! I could not have completed the book without your energy, intelligence, and hard work. Thank you for your brilliance.

Third, thanks to my brother Patrick Cashman, sister Karen Cashman, and my cousin Jerry Cashman for your loving support, and more important your caring honesty in offering critical feedback after reading the draft manuscript. I am so grateful for your generosity, love, and clear guidance. Thanks for better aligning my voice and message.

Next, I thank my wonderful clients and colleagues over the course of my career. You inspire me and teach me daily. Being able to witness the growth of CEOs and senior executives is a privilege I never take for granted. You let me live my purpose and for that I am ever aware and ever grateful.

The client and expert interviews we conducted for this book were crucial to breathing life into it. Although there were many from whom we learned, we offer special thanks to Daniel Vasella, Michael Paxton, Ludwig Hantson, Deborah Dunsire, Paul Laudicina, Laura Karet, Richard Leider,

Terry Bacon, Marc Belton, Mark Addicks, Rohinish Hooda, Jeff George, Vas Navasimhan, Karen Kimsey-House, Pablo Gaito, Jeannine McGlade, Andrew Pek, Steve Piersanti, Jane Stevenson, Ken Shelton, Ron James, Tom Morgan, Dave Moen, David Rothenberger, and Chip Conley. You stimulated us with your insights and examples and inspired us to think and see the book in new ways.

Thanks to Warren Bennis, whom I consider the godfather of leadership development and the embodiment of leadership presence. Warren's memoir, *Still Surprised*, moved me greatly while working on this book. I acknowledge his influential work and that of Clayton Christenson, Jeff Dyer, Hal Gregerson, Tom Kelley, Peter Senge, Bill George, Otto Scharmer, Daniel Goleman, Daniel Kahneman, Timothy Wilson, Susan Cain, Richard Leider, Ram Charan, Terry Bacon, Margaret Wheatley, Bob Johansen, Jim Collins, Jerry Porras, Thomas Friedman, David Brooks, Daniel Pink, and others whom I hope I have remembered in this book's bibliography.

Thanks to everyone at Berrett-Koehler Publishers, the finest publishing partners an author could be privileged to have: Steve Piersanti, Jeevan Simvasubramaniam, Neal Maillet, Johanna Vondeling, Richard Wilson, Dianne Platner, Kristen Franz, Michael Crowley, David Marshall, Cynthia Shannon, and the rest of your mission-driven team including Linda Jupiter and her creative, tenacious production and design professionals.

We are very grateful to our public relations and social media experts Barbara Cave Henricks, Rusty Shelton, and Jessica Krakoski. Your vision, experience, energy, and creative talent matched your authenticity and consummate professionalism.

Thanks for the careful readings and keen insights of reviewers and colleagues Ulf Wolf, Mike McNair, Andrea Chilcote, Peter Bridges, Corey Seitz, Mark Moshier, Johannes Shubmehl, and Jacqueline Byrd. You gave us valuable, fresh perspective.

Deep thanks to my colleagues at Korn/Ferry, especially to Terry Bacon for his support and recent, well-researched books on power and influence. Your combination of intelligence and collaboration is a special thing to experience. Special thanks to Gary Burnison, Bob Eichinger, Ana Dutra,

Mary Beth Barron, Kim Ruyle, Evelyn Orr, Lewis Rusen, Scott Kingdom, Joe Griesedieck, Jane Stevenson, Janet Feldman, Dee Gaeddert, Carissa Lund, Sue Puncochar, Lee Artimovich, Ken DeMeuse, Bill McCarthy, Christoph la Garde, Nancy Atwood, Jeff Rosenthal, Peter Thies, Renee Garpestad, Dina Rauker, Anne Tessien, Craig Sneltjes, Elizabeth Gaito, Kate Smith, Joanne Flesner, Sama Sandy, Lindsay DeRosia, Jenny French, John Pike, Ryan Hill, Joan Davis, and all the rest of my colleagues for your support and creative collaboration over the years.

I express profound gratitude to two of my spiritual mentors. Maharishi Mahesh Yogi passed a few years ago, but his great knowledge and wisdom lives on. Chunyi Lin, qigong master, guides me regularly to deep silence with the kind of love, presence, and depth that I can only aspire to attain someday. You are the pause principle in action.

Profound thanks to my dearest uncle, Gene Cashman, who passed during the writing of this book after a rich, service-filled life of ninety-one years. Gene was successful in business, but even more successful in life. His passion for people, his riveting presence, and his continuous love of service lives on in all of us. Gene, we will pause it forward as best we can!

The ultimate gratitude goes to you, the reader. Thanks for bringing life to the book by pausing deeply and making a purposeful difference in your life and in the lives of all the people you touch. I wrote this book for brave, authentic leaders like you, who have the courage to pause, envision, and commit to the new and the different, and in so doing transform lives. Thank you for the privilege and honor of inviting me, and this book, into your life.

INDEX

A. T. Kearney, 24
Addicks, Mark, 103, 119–20
Africa, 14, 55, 131
agility, 6, 9
Aha!/Eureka! moments, 11, 68, 71, 108
Allen, David, 16
ambiguity, 6, 9, 25, 109. *See also* creativity
American Psychological Association, 46
Anderson, Ray, 111–14, 118, 132
Apple, 22, 23, 25, 58–59, 68,
    108–10, 112, 127
Army War College, 6
Art of Powerful Questions, The (Vogt et al.),
    21, 86–87
Arthur, W. Brian, 13–14, 17
Augustine, St., 43
authenticity
    as "being your talk," 49
    character and, 49, 51
    credibility based on, 30, 34–35
    factors in, 5
    and growth of others, 80, 105–6
    innovation and, 129
    listening with, 33, 88–90
    pause it forward with, 132
    Pause Principle on, 34–35, 75–76,
        105–6
    and personal leadership growth, 41, 43,
        49, 75–76, 103
    "purpose moment" and, 14
    of questions, 86–88
    self–awareness and, 10, 20–21, 41, 43, 75
    value creation and, 34
awareness in others, 94–95. *See also*
    self-awareness

"Back to the Rhythm" expedition, 14
backwards pause, 119. *See also* pause
Bacon, Terry, 30, 46, 48
Barton, Michelle A., 12–13, 90
Baxter Bioscience, 26

BDNF (brain-derived neurotrophic factor),
    66
Beating the Global Odds (Laudicina), 24–25
"being our talk", 49. *See also* authenticity
Belton, Marc, 102–3, 119–20
Bennis, Warren, 6, 33, 42, 57, 96
Berkana Institute, 131
Berrett-Koehler Publishers, 15, 121–22,
    167–68
bias for action, 91
Bierce, Ambrose, 51–52
BIG–Biosurgery Idea Gurus, 16, 123
Bill & Melinda Gates Foundation, 131
BookExpo America, 1–2
boredom, 90–91
brain functioning. *See also* mind; thinking
    creativity and, 11, 72
    exercise and, 66
    hemispheres of brain, 71–72
    "intelligent memory" of, 71
    meditation and, 69–70
    naps and, 66
brain-derived neurotrophic factor (BDNF),
    66
Brazil, 18–19
Breaking Away (Stevenson and Kaafarani),
    113–14
"Brief" pause practice before surgery, 15–16
Brokatsky-Geiger, Juergen, 101
Brooks, David, 44
Brown, Juanita, 21, 86–87
Byron, Lord, 72

Cargill, 16
caring directness, 77–79, 126. *See also*
    emotional intelligence
Casals, Pablo, 98
Cashman, Kevin
    at Army War College, 6
    at BookExpo America, 1–2
    books by, 17–18, 41, 163

career of, 163–64
consulting firm of, 31
core purpose of, 63, 64
and ethical transformations in CEO
    leadership, 132
health crisis in family of, 31–32
and hitting the VUCA wall, 31–32
and pause it forward, 132
Pause Sanctuary in home of, 32
travel to India by, 18
wife and son of, 18, 31–32, 164
and writing *The Pause Principle*, 17–18
Youth Frontiers and, 132, 164
Cashman, Soraya, 18, 31
Caux Roundtable, 132, 164
Center for Creative Leadership, 25
Center for Ethical Business Cultures,
    University of St. Thomas, 8, 132, 164
Center for Mindfulness in Medicine, Health
    Care, and Society, 69
CFA (Character Foundation Assessment), 48
Chamilia, 15, 115
change. *See also* growth of others; growth of
personal leadership; innovation
    and becoming the leader one wishes to
      see in others, 84–85, 105–6
    beginning of, in self-change, 84
    for collaborative leadership style, 93
    as constant of leadership, 68
    trauma as change-producing teacher, 96
character. *See also* courage; humility; wisdom
    authenticity and, 49, 51
    battle between being self-serving and
      serving others, 51–52
    character-driven leadership, 30
    coping versus, 50–53
    definition of, 46
    Emerson on, 46, 50
    energy benefit of, 54
    Leading in Character versus Leading by
      Coping, 50–54
    list of character strengths, 47, 53
    Pause Points on, 47, 54
    power of, 46, 54–55
    self-assessment tools on, 47, 48
    self-awareness and, 41
    study of, 46–49
    values and, 55–58
    of youth, 132

Character Foundation Assessment (CFA), 48
Character Strengths and Virtues (Peterson and
    Seligman), 46–47
Charan, Ram, 79
Charlie Rose Brain Series, 71
Cheerios, 119–20
Chief Executive Institute, 17, 40, 164
Chihuly, Dale, 81
China, 79
Christensen, Clayton, 22, 123
Chuang Tzu, vi
Chunyi Lin, 72
Church, Allan, 39
Churchill, Winston, 103
Churchland, Patricia, 71
Cicero, 42
clarity out of complexity, 6, 9, 24–28, 33
Climate Reality Project, 131
Clinton Health Access Initiative, 131
Clooney, George, 96
Coaches Training Institute, 16, 81–82
collaboration
    change in leadership style for, 39
    "connect and collaborate" system, 93
    for innovation, 110–11, 115–16, 119–20
    listening and, 89
Collins, Jim, 41, 81
"command and control" system, 93
commitment in others, 95–97
complexity, 6, 9. *See also* VUCA forces
    clarity out of, 24–28, 33
Conaty, Bill, 79
Confucius, 51
conscious versus unconscious mind, 71–72
Coolidge, Calvin, 89
Cooper, Thomas, 25
coping, 50–53
core purpose, 61–65. *See also* purpose
Cornell University, 39
Corporate Executive Board, 82
courage
    as character strength, 47, 48, 50, 53
    for growth of others, 96
    for reflection, 81
    for risking experimentation, 33, 115, 116
Coyle, Daniel, 98
Cray, Seymour, 116
Cray Research, 116

creativity. *See also* imagination; innovation; inventors
  Aha!/Eureka! moments, 11, 68, 71, 108
  ambiguity and, 25
  brain functioning and, 11, 71, 72
  as character strength, 47, 48
  cross-disciplinary ideas and, 123
  curiosity and, 123
  freedom and, 11
  and growth of others, 82, 83, 103, 124–25
  listening and, 88
  meditation and, 69
  pause and, 9–12, 18, 80, 107, 124–25, 126
  questioning and, 21, 33, 86–87
  transcendental pause and, 69, 70
credibility
  of leaders, 30, 34–35, 83–84, 87
  of managers, 67
cross-disciplinary ideas, 123
Csikszentmihalyi, Mihaly, 70
cultures of innovation. *See* innovation
curiosity, 123, 128. *See also* questioning

Dalai Lama, 18
Darwin, Charles, 109
de Gaulle, Charles, 54–55
deep practice, 98
deep/transcendental pause, 66–73, 99–101
"democratization of information," 93
Descendants, The, 96
discovery skills, 22
Disney, 23
Drawing on the Right Side of the Brain (Edwards), 72
drive
  balancing care and, 77–79
  balancing immediate drive with future innovation, 125–26
  harnessing of, through pause, 30–31
  innovative cultures as purpose-driven, 111–15
  of leaders, 30
  of managers, 4–5, 38–39, 45
  to pause, 26
  service-driven approach, 5, 30, 51–52, 71, 121–22
Duggan, William, 71
Dunsire, Deborah, 56–57
Dyer, Jeff, 22, 87, 123

Ecology of Commerce, The (Hawken), 112
Edison, Thomas, 110
Edwards, Betty, 71–72
Eichinger, Bob, 25
Einstein, Albert, 12, 46, 57, 68, 107–8, 109, 110
Einstein: His Life and Universe (Isaacson), 108
Elements of Influence, The (Bacon), 30
Elements of Power, The (Bacon), 30, 46, 48
Emerson, Ralph Waldo, 46, 50
emotional intelligence, 43, 51, 67, 78, 91, 96. *See also* caring directness
Erikson, Erik, 102
ethical behavior, 8, 49, 51–52, 132. *See also headings beginning with* value
Ethicon Biosurgery, Johnson & Johnson, 16, 122–23
Eureka!/Aha! moments, 11, 68, 71, 108
executive development. *See* growth of personal leadership
Executive to Leader Institute, 17
exercise, 11, 66, 73
experimentation, risk of, 33, 74, 104, 109, 116–17, 128. *See also* innovation
"eye of the needle" metaphor, 92

Facebook, 125
failure and innovation, 116–17. *See also* risk of experimentation
Fairview Health System, 15–16
fast versus slow thinking, 8–9, 22
fear
  courage from, 96
  deep pause and, 73
  of failure, 116–17
  and growth of others, 89, 91, 96, 99
  hesitation and, 28–29
  and Leading by Coping, 50, 53
  listening to others' fears, 89, 91
  pause for dealing with, 80
firefighters, 12–13
Fishman, Mark, 109
"Five-Minute Synchronization," 16
"flow," 70
Folkman, Joe, 41
forward pause, 119, 120. *See also* pause
Francis, St., 91
freedom
  creativity and, 11
  innovation and, 109
  pause and, 28

Friedman, Thomas, 93

Gaito, Pablo, 16
Gameful, 131
Gandhi, Mahatma, 72, 82
Gates, Bill and Melinda, 131
General Mills, 102–3, 119–20
generative listening, 93–94. *See also* listening
generativity, 34, 75, 102–3, 105, 129, 132
George, Bill, 42
George, Jeff, 16, 125–26
Get There Early (Johansen), 6
Giant Eagle, 59–61
Gilbert, Daniel, 71
global issues, 51, 93, 131–32. *See also*
    VUCA forces
Goleman, Daniel, 41, 42
Good to Great (Collins), 81
Google, 23, 24, 66, 125, 127
Gopnik, Alison, 44
Green Bay Packers, 77–78
Green Peak Partners, 39
Gregersen, Hal, 22, 87, 123
growth. *See also* growth of others; growth of
    personal leadership
    as core purpose, 63
    domains of, 20
    as external process, 83
    not growing versus, 20–21
    questions on, 19, 83
growth of cultures of innovation. *See*
    innovation
growth of others
    acceleration of, 99
    authenticity and, 80, 105–6
    building awareness and, 94–95
    building commitment and, 95–97
    building practice and, 97–99
    and care balanced with drive, 77–79
    continuous process of, 83–86
    deep pause for, 99–101
    generativity and, 102–3, 105
    and inside–out/outside–in dynamics,
        101, 105
    language of, 86–94
    leader's role in catalyzing human
        potential, 82, 83
    and less as more, 79–81
    listening and, 86, 88–99, 104
    merging interrelated pauses for, 94–99

    at Novartis, 99–101
    Pause Points on, 85–86, 88, 99, 102, 106
    Pause Practices on, 103–6
    purpose and, 103–4
    questioning and, 86–88, 94–99, 104
    and reflection and synthesis, 104–5
    risking experimentation and, 104
    and self-confidence balanced with
        humility, 91–92
    self-growth before, 20–21, 84–85, 105–6
    synergy and, 81–82
    visioning of, 106
growth of personal leadership. *See also* leaders
    authenticity and, 41, 43, 49, 75–76, 103
    and change as constant of leadership, 68
    character and, 46–55
    core purpose and, 61–65
    generativity and, 75
    growth of whole person for, 37–41
    and inside–out/outside–in dynamics,
        44–45, 75
    Pause Points on, 40, 43–44, 47, 53–54,
        57–58, 63–65, 72–73, 76
    Pause Practices on, 74–76
    purpose and, 58–65, 74
    and questioning and listening, 74
    reflection and synthesis for, 33–34, 39,
        74–75, 104–5, 128
    restorative pause and, 66
    risking experimentation and, 74
    self-awareness and, 38, 39, 41–44, 75,
        94–95, 103
    self-growth before growth of others,
        20–21, 84–85, 105–6
    transcendental/deep pause and, 66–73
    unlocking leadership potential, 40
    values clarification and, 55–58
    visioning of, 76

Häagen-Dazs, 15, 115–16
Habitat for Humanity, 131
Hadza, 55
Hamlet (Shakespeare), 49
Hantson, Ludwig, 26
Harvard University, 71, 108
Hawken, Paul, 112
Healing of the Mind series (PBS), 69–70
hesitation, 28–30
Hoffman, Banesh, 107
Hooda, Rohinish, 16, 122–23

How: Why How We Do Anything Means Everything (Seidman), 93
human resources. *See* growth of others
humanity, 47, 48. *See also* service-driven approach
humility
    as character strength, 47, 48, 53
    drive balanced with, 30
    listening with, 91–92
    pause and, 81
    self-confidence balanced with, for growth of others, 91–92
    "situated humility," 13
    and wisdom of experience, 5
hyperactive state, 2, 11, 26, 27, 91, 122, 125. *See also* VUCA forces
hypoactive state, 27

image of leaders, 50–51
imagination, 11–12, 108. *See also* creativity; innovation; visioning
Imagine: How Creativity Works (Lehrer), 11–12
impatience, 90–91
India, 18
influence of leaders, 30, 50–51, 89
inner knowing, 13–14, 17. *See also* knowledge; wisdom
innovation. *See also specific innovators and companies*
    and ambiguity and uncertainty, 109
    authenticity and, 129
    balancing immediate drive with future innovation, 125–26
    boldness and, 108–9
    breaking through boundaries to, 124–25
    collaboration for, 110–11, 115–16, 119–20
    creating culture of, 115–16
    and creation of new normal, 7–9
    curiosity and, 123, 128
    domains of, 117–18
    and growth of others, 83
    inside-out/outside in forces shaping, 114–15, 129
    invention and, 109–11
    listening and, 89, 114, 128
    missions to move innovation, 121–22
    as new leadership, 23, 111
    Pause Points on, 114–15, 118, 129–30
    and power of "Why?," 122–23

purpose and, 111–15, 118, 128
    questioning and, 22, 87, 114, 119–20, 122–23
    by risking experimentation and failure, 109, 116–17, 128
    self-awareness and, 110
    self-innovation, 117–18
    shifting focus and opening up possibilities for, 126–27
    skills of innovators, 22
    types of, 114
    value creation and, 110–11
    visioning culture of, 129–30
Innovator's DNA, The (Christensen et al.), 22, 87
inside-out/outside-in dynamics
    and growth of others, 101, 105
    and growth of personal leadership, 44–45, 75
    of innovation, 114–15, 129
    Pause Point on, 114–15
    Pause Principle on, 34, 75, 105, 113, 129
    self-awareness and, 44–45
insight. See *Aha!/Eureka!* moments; creativity
Interface, Inc., 111–13
International Development Enterprises, 132
inventors, 109–11. *See also* innovation
Isaacs, David, 21, 86–87
Isaacson, Walter, 108

James, Ron, 8
Jobs, Steve
    death of, 23
    and fonts for Macintosh, 68
    as innovator, 22, 23, 108, 109–10, 112
    pause and, 25
    purpose of, 58–59
    questioning skills of, 22
Johansen, Bob, 6
Johansson, Frans, 123
Johnson & Johnson, 16, 122–23
justice/civic strengths, 47, 48

Kaafarani, Bilal, 113–14
Kabat-Zinn, Jon, 69–71
Kahneman, Daniel, 8
Kandel, Erik, 71
Karet, Laura, 59–61
Kimsey-House, Karen, 16, 81–82

knowledge. *See also* wisdom
    accessibility of, 24
    as character strength, 47, 48
    geometric expansion of, 24–25
    knowledge work, 21
Korn/Ferry International, 30, 31, 48, 113,
    164

"lantern consciousness," 44
Lao-Tzu, 43, 97, 133
Laudicina, Paul, 24–25
Law of Thermodynamics, second, 7
leaders. *See also* authenticity; growth of
        others; growth of personal leadership;
        innovation; pause; *and specific leaders*
    character of, 30, 46–55
    coping by, 50–53
    creation of future by, 67, 127
    credibility of, 30, 34–35, 83–84, 87
    dealing with ambiguity by, 25, 109
    drive of, 30
    evolution from managers to, 14–15, 27
    failure of new organizational leaders, 89
    flipping VUCA forces by, 6–10, 13, 25,
        26, 87
    generativity and, 34, 75, 102–3, 105,
        129, 132
    going beyond competition by, 116
    growth questions for, 83
    influence and image of, 30, 50–51, 89
    innovation and, 23, 30, 109, 110–11
    managers versus, 3–5, 13–15, 22, 27–28,
        30, 33, 35, 38–39, 45, 49, 57, 67,
        71, 74, 79, 82, 83, 92, 116, 127, 128
    people-centered, service-driven approach
        by, 5, 30, 51–52, 71, 79, 121–22, 126
    pressures and stresses on, 4–5
    risking experimentation by, 33, 74, 104,
        109, 116–17, 128
Leaders Make the Future (Johansen), 6
Leadership and Talent Consulting, 31
Leadership Architect (Korn/Ferry), 48
leadership development. *See* growth of
        others; growth of personal leadership
leadership development audit, 85–86
Leadership from the Inside Out (Cashman),
    41, 163
LeaderSource Ltd., 31, 164
Leading by Coping, 50–53
Leading in Character, 50–54

Lehrer, Jonah, 11–12
Leider, Richard, 14, 55
less as more, 79–81
"Level V Leaders," 81
Lincoln, Abraham, 55
listening. *See also* questioning
    authentic listening, 33, 88–90
    for building commitment, 95–97
    for building practice, 97–99
    "eye of the needle" metaphor for, 92
    generative listening, 93–94
    for growth of others, 86, 88–99, 104
    for growth of personal leadership, 74
    innovation and, 89, 114, 128
    pitfalls of, 90–91
    power of, 88–91, 93–94
    questions with or without authentic
        listening, 89
    as receptive language of pause, 33, 74,
        104
    research on lack of, 89–90
    and self-confidence balanced with
        humility, 91–92
    synergy and, 92
    in VUCA world, 93–94
Lombardi, Vince, 77–78
Lombardo, Michael, 25
Lominger International, 25, 31
Lore International, 30, 31
love, 56, 77–79, 126. *See also* humanity;
        service-driven approach
LRN, 93

managers
    answers found by, 128
    competency of, 45
    credibility of, 67
    decision making by, 33–34, 57
    dependability and accuracy of, 22, 35
    drive and control asserted by, 4–5, 83
    efficiency and speed of, 28, 30, 67, 82,
        109
    ethical behavior enforced by, 49
    evolution of, to leaders, 14–15, 27
    failure avoided by, 117
    and future directions of organization,
        127
    goals pursued by, as Human Doers, 71
    and keeping pace with competition, 116

managers *(continued)*
  leaders versus, 3–5, 13–15, 22, 27–28,
    30, 33, 35, 38–39, 45, 49, 57, 67,
    71, 74, 79, 82, 83, 92, 116, 127, 128
  people perceived as resource by, 79
  as results-driven, 38–39, 45, 74, 82
  risk minimized by, 33
  self-driven management and, 30
  stimulus/response pattern of, 126
  well-formulated, time-tested approaches
    by, 13
Mandela, Nelson, 72
Maslow, Abraham, 70
May, Rollo, 28
McGill, Bryant, 61
McGlade, Jeannine, 124–25
McGonigal, Jane, 131
media, 25
"Medici Effect," 123
meditation, 11, 16, 32, 66, 69–73, 126
Medtronic, 42, 109–10
Melrose, Ken, 117
midlife crisis, 62
Millennium Pharmaceutical, 56–57
Milner, Brenda, 71
mind. *See also* brain functioning; thinking
  conscious versus unconscious mind,
    71–72
mindfulness, 69–70, 72–73
Mindfulness-based Stress Reduction
    program, 69
mission. *See also* purpose
  for moving innovation, 121–22
  organizational versus personal mission, 61
mission pause, 119–20. *See also* pause
MIT, 108
MIT Sloan Management Review, 12–13, 90
Morrison, Elizabeth Wolfe, 89
Moyers, Bill, 69–70
Mozart, Wolfgang Amadeus, 11
music, 72, 73, 98
myelin, 98

Namaste (expression of honor and respect), 60
naps, 66
Narasimhan, Vas, 43
Neuron, 71
New York Times, 16, 93
NIBR (Novartis Institute Biomedical
    Research), 108–9

Nike, 66
non-doing, 70–71
nosce teipsum (Know thyself), 42
Novartis, 6, 28, 38, 43, 99–101, 108–9
Novartis Institute Biomedical Research
    (NIBR), 108–9

Onward (Schultz), 62
openness, 79–80
*Organizational Behavior and Human
    Decision Process* (See et al.), 89
Orr, Evelyn, 48
outside-in/inside-out dynamics. *See* inside
    out/outside-in dynamics
Ovid, 42

Page, Larry, 125
partnership. *See* collaboration
pause. *See also* growth of others; growth of
    personal leadership; innovation;
    leaders; Pause Points; Pause Principle
  backwards pause, 119
  big *P* Pause, 69–73
  and clarity out of complexity, 24–28
  consequences of losing or giving up
    practice of, 31–32
  and continuous reflection and action
    loop, 12–13
  and creation of new normal, 7–9
  creativity and, 11–12
  drive to pause, 26
  and evolution from managers to leaders,
    14–15
  examples of pragmatic pause, 15–17
  fighting fires with, 12–13
  flipping VUCA forces through, 6–10,
    13, 25, 26, 87
  forward pause, 119, 120
  for global issues, 131–32
  harnessing drive through, 30–31
  hesitation versus, 28–30
  as inherent, generative principle, 18, 126
  inner knowing and, 13–14, 17
  for leading forward, 3–5
  listening as receptive language of, 33,
    74, 104
  long pause, 17–18
  mission pause, 119–20
  as "purpose moment," 14
  purposeful performance and, 2, 8–11

question on pausing versus not pausing, 19–20, 28

questions as language of, 21–22, 23, 33, 74, 104

restorative pause, 66

Seven Pause Practices, 32–36

transcendental/deep pause, 66–73, 99–101

wisdom of experience and, 5

pause it forward, 132

Pause Points. *See also* pause; Pause Principle

accelerating growth of others, 99

alignment to core purpose, 64–65

character pattern, 47

deep pause, 72–73

developing others, 102

distilling own purpose, 63–64

on growth of others, 85–86, 88, 99, 102, 106

on growth of personal leadership, 40, 43–44, 47, 53–54, 57–58, 63–65, 72–73, 76

on innovation, 114–15, 118, 129–30

inside-out/outside in forces shaping innovation, 114–15

leadership development audit, 85–86

leading by coping, 53

Leading in Character, 54

moving from hesitation to pause to deliberate action, 29–30

pause to perform, 10–11

power of questions, 88

purpose-fueled innovation, 118

purpose of, 9–10

self-awareness, 43–44

unlocking leadership potential, 40

values clarification, 57–58

visioning culture of innovation, 129–30

visioning growth of others, 106

visioning personal leadership growth, 76

Pause Principle. *See also* pause; Pause Points

on authenticity, 34–35, 75–76, 105–6, 129

on being on–purpose, 33, 74, 103–4, 128

definition of, 7–8

on generativity, 34, 75, 105, 129

for growth of cultures of innovation, 128–29

for growth of others, 103–6

for growth of personal leadership, 74–76

growth principles underlying, 20

on inside–out/outside–in dynamics, 34, 75, 105, 113, 129

model of, 26–27

purpose of, 37

on questioning and listening, 33, 74, 104, 128

on reflection and synthesis, 33–34, 74–75, 104–5, 128

on risking experimentation, 33, 74, 104, 128

Seven Pause Practices, 32–36

as universal, 7

Pause Principle, The (Cashman), 17–18

Paxton, Mike, 15, 115–16

"peak experiences," 70

Peirce Group, 48

Pek, Andrew, 124–25

performance. *See also* growth of others; growth of personal leadership; innovation

pause for purposeful performance, 2, 8–11

self-awareness of high performers, 39

personal leadership. *See* growth of personal leadership

Peterson, Christopher, 46–47

Piersanti, Steve, 15, 121–22

Pillsbury, 15, 115

Pillsbury Doughboy, 115

Pink, Dan, 71–72

Pixar, 23

Polak, Paul, 132

power

of character, 46, 54–55

"command and control" system of, 93

"connect and collaborate" system of, 93

corruption by, 51–52

of listening, 88–91, 93–94

personal sources of, 46

of questions, 86–88, 122–23

of synergy, 81–82

power naps, 66

Power of Purpose, The (Leider), 14

practice, 97–99

prayer, 72, 73, 121

"presencing," 70

Presencing Institute, 131–32

Procter & Gamble, 59, 127

purpose
    being on-purpose, 33, 74, 103–4, 128
    benefits of clarifying, 61
    core purpose, 61–65
    distilling of, 63–64
    getting to heart of, 59–62
    and growth of others, 103–4
    innovation and, 111–15, 118, 128
    Leider on "purpose moment," 14
    pause it forward with, 132
    Pause Points on, 63–65, 118
    and personal leadership growth, 58–65,
        74
    self-awareness and, 41
    as transformative force of leadership,
        56–62

qigong, 72, 73
questioning. See also listening; Pause Points
    authentic listening and, 89
    aversion to, in current culture, 21
    for building awareness in others, 95
    for building commitment, 95–97
    for building practice, 97–99
    for growth of others, 86–88, 88, 94–99,
        104
    for growth of personal leadership, 74
    innovation and, 22, 87, 114, 119–20,
        122–23, 128
    knowledge work and, 21
    as language of pause, 21–22, 23, 33, 74,
        104
    by leaders versus managers, 22
    power of, 86–88, 122–23
    VUCA forces and, 87
    "Why?" as powerful question, 122–23

reflection and action loop, 12–13
reflection and synthesis, 33–34, 39, 74–75,
    104–5, 128
restorative pause, 66
retreats, 11, 14, 16, 26, 32
risk of experimentation, 33, 74, 104, 109,
    116–17, 128. See also innovation
Rollwagen, John, 116
Rothenberger, David, 15–16
Rothman, Naomi, 89
Ruyle, Kim, 48
Salesforce.com, 127
Sandoz, 16, 125–26

Santa Fe Institute, 13
São Paulo, Brazil, 18–19
Scharmer, Otto, 70, 110
Schultz, Howard, 62
"search-light consciousness," 44
See, Kelly, 89
Seidman, Dov, 93
self-awareness. See also awareness in others
    authenticity and, 10, 20–21, 41, 43, 75
    benefits of, 41–42
    as classic theme, 42–43
    continuous loop of, 44–45
    innovation and, 110
    inside-out/outside-in dynamics of, 44–45
    Pause Point on, 43–44
    performance and, 39
    personal leadership growth and, 38, 39,
        41–44, 75, 94–95, 103
self-confidence, 90, 91–92
Seligman, Martin, 46–47
Seneca, 85
Senge, Peter, 70, 92, 93–94
service-driven approach, 5, 30, 51–52, 71,
    121–22
Seven Pause Practices, 32–36
Seven Sages of Greece, 42
Shakespeare, William, 49
Shapira, David, 59
Shaw, George Bernard, 52
"situated humility," 13
sleep, 3, 12, 66
slow versus fast thinking, 8–9, 22
Social Animal, The (Brooks), 44
Socrates, 42
Soll, Jack, 89
Sperry, Roger, 71
Spring Forest Qigong, 72
Squire, Larry, 71
staff development. See growth of others
Starbucks, 62
Stephanopoulos, George, 1, 2
Stevenson, Jane, 113–14
stewardship model, 122
Stimulated! (McGlade and Pek), 124–25
stimulus/pause/multiple responses, 126
stimulus/response pattern, 126
Strangers to Ourselves (Wilson), 71, 72
surmenage, 3
sustainability, 111–13

Sutcliffe, Kathleen M., 12–13, 90
synergy, 81–82, 92
synthesis, 33–34, 74–75, 104–5, 128

tai chi, 73
Takeda Oncology Company, 56–57
Talent Code, The (Coyle), 98
talent development. *See* growth of others
Talent Masters, The (Conaty), 79
Talmud, 37
Tanzania, 14, 55
Tao Te Ching (Lao-Tzu), 97
Taoism, 70, 79
"TED in the head," 123
temperance, 47, 48
Theory U (Scharmer), 70, 110
thinking. *See also* brain functioning; mind
    fast thinking versus slow thinking, 8–9,
        22
    intelligent actions beginning with, 30
Thinking, Fast and Slow (Kahneman), 8
Tichy, Noel, 96
TM (Transcendental Meditation), 69
Toro, 117
transactive state, 27
transcendence, 47, 48, 66–73, 99–101. *See
    also* innovation
Transcendental Meditation (TM), 69
transformative state, 27
True North (George), 42

unconscious versus conscious mind, 71–72
understanding, 6, 9
University of California–Berkeley, 66
University of Illinois–Champaign, 66
University of Massachusetts Medical School,
    69
University of Minnesota, 15–16
University of St. Thomas, Center for Ethical
    Business Cultures, 8, 132, 164
University of Virginia, 71
unpredictability, 6, 9

value creation
    authenticity and, 34
    and growth of others, 82
    innovation and, 110–11

values clarification, 55–58
Values in Action (VIA) Institute on
    Character, 46–47, 48
Vasella, Daniel, 6, 28, 38, 108–9
VIA (Values in Action) Institute on
    Character, 46–47, 48
vision, 6, 9
visioning
    of culture of innovation, 129–30
    of growth of others, 106
    of personal leadership growth, 76
Vogt, Eric, 21, 86–87
volatility, 6, 9
VUCA forces
    and efficiency versus innovation, 109
    hitting the VUCA wall, 31–32, 38
    leaders' flipping of, through pause, 6–10,
        13, 25, 26, 87
    listening and, 93–94
    meaning of, 6
    questioning and, 87

W. Warner Burke Associates, 39
Walker, Mathew, 66
walking, 11, 66, 73
Walser-Ertel, Mechtild, 100
Wheatley, Margaret, 30, 131
Whole New Mind, A (Pink), 71–72
"Why?" question, 122–23. *See also*
    questioning
Wilson, Timothy, 71, 72
wisdom
    attitude of, 5, 13
    as character strength, 47, 48
    of experience, 5
    inner knowing and, 13–14, 17
Wozniak, Steve, 58–59
writing, 15, 17–18, 32, 63, 121, 124
Wu Wei (principle of least action), 79

yoga, 60, 73
Youth Frontiers, 132, 164

Zenger, Jack, 41
"zone," 70, 81
Zuckerberg, Mark, 125

ABOUT THE AUTHOR

Kevin Cashman is recognized as one of the pioneering thought leaders in leadership development and executive coaching and is regarded as one of the world's premier CEO coaches. *Leadership Excellence* magazine has named him one of the Top 10 Thought Leaders for several years. For more than thirty years, he has advised senior executives and senior teams in more than sixty countries. Cashman has authored six leadership books, including two business book bestsellers. *Leadership from the Inside Out*, first published in 1998, is considered a business classic, was listed as one of the top-selling business books of the decade by CEO-READ, and the #1 Bestselling Business Book of 2000. The second edition, published in 2008, is currently used at more than 100 universities and leadership programs worldwide.

Cashman is often identified as "the personal leadership guru" for his multifaceted, interdisciplinary approaches to "grow the whole person to grow the whole leader." He is a frequent keynote speaker at leadership development events at corporations, universities, and associations. He has been featured in *Forbes*, *Fast Company*, the *Wall Street Journal*, *strategy+leadership*, CNN and other media sources. Kevin founded the Chief Executive Institute and LeaderSource Ltd., recognized as one of the top three leadership firms globally. In 2006, LeaderSource and the Chief Executive Institute joined Korn/Ferry International, where he serves as senior partner, CEO and Executive Development. His distinguished list of clients is a "who's who" of the most admired companies in the world. Many have engaged Kevin for continuous advisory service through multiple leadership succession changes that have spanned a decade or two.

Cashman holds a degree in psychology from St. John's University and is an adjunct professor for the University of Minnesota Executive Education program.

He is a Senior Fellow in the Caux Roundtable, a consortium of CEOs dedicated to principle-centered leadership. He is also a board member of the Center for Ethical Business Cultures at the University of St. Thomas and a former board member for Youth Frontiers, which serves the character development of 120,000 students annually.

A believer in both pause and dynamic action, Cashman has practiced and taught meditation over four decades, and although retired from competition now, he has competed in more than seventy triathlons. Living in Minneapolis with his spouse, Soraya, and their son, Tahiel, Kevin aspires to someday be as loving, affectionate and happy as their Golden Retriever, Leo.

For more information, go to www.CashmanLeadership.com, where you can access the most current thinking, resources and best practices related to leadership transformation, as well as information on Kevin's coaching, advisory services, and keynote speaking.

Berrett–Koehler
Publishers

A community dedicated to creating
a world that works for all

Visit Our Website: www.bkconnection.com

Read book excerpts, see author videos and Internet movies, read our authors' blogs, join discussion groups, download book apps, find out about the BK Affiliate Network, browse subject-area libraries of books, get special discounts, and more!

Subscribe to Our Free E-Newsletter, the *BK Communiqué*

Be the first to hear about new publications, special discount offers, exclusive articles, news about bestsellers, and more! Get on the list for our free e-newsletter by going to **www.bkconnection.com**.

Get Quantity Discounts

Berrett-Koehler books are available at quantity discounts for orders of ten or more copies. Please call us toll-free at (800) 929-2929 or email us at bkp .orders@aidcvt.com.

Join the BK Community

BKcommunity.com is a virtual meeting place where people from around the world can engage with kindred spirits to create a world that works for all. BKcommunity.com members may create their own profiles, blog, start and participate in forums and discussion groups, post photos and videos, answer surveys, announce and register for upcoming events, and chat with others online in real time. Please join the conversation!